ALEXANDRIA
A City & Myth

ALEXANDRIA
A City & Myth

NIALL FINNERAN

TEMPUS

First published 2005

Tempus Publishing Limited
The Mill, Brimscombe Port,
Stroud, Gloucestershire, GL5 2QG
www.tempus-publishing.com

British Library Cataloguing in Publication Data.
A catalogue record for this book is available from the British Library.

ISBN 0 7524 3341 5

Typesetting and origination by Tempus Publishing Limited
Printed in Great Britain

CONTENTS

ACKNOWLEDGEMENTS

This book was partly written when I was a British Academy Postdoctoral Research Fellow at the University of London's School of Oriental and African Studies (SOAS), and latterly as a lecturer in the Department of Archaeology and the Centre for Antiquity and Middle Ages, School of Humanities, University of Southampton. My thanks go to many colleagues and students, past and present, for their part in helping shape my research, as well as the British Academy and SOAS for the financial support that enabled me to visit Alexandria and visit first-hand all the major locations described herein. Special mention goes to the patient staff of the libraries of SOAS, University of Southampton, the Society of Antiquaries of London – especially Adrian James – and last but certainly not least the Egypt Exploration Society, where the librarian Chris Naunton deserves special praise for his unfailing help and patience with late returns. Special thanks, for various help and assistance rendered, goes to the following individuals listed below, some of whom are involved with me on a new and exciting second stage of research in Alexandria, mapping the urban landscape; in a sense this book is just a starting point, a manifesto of ideas, we now must move further and it is anticipated that a new programme of urban archaeological survey will yield results that will (hopefully!) make some of the statements outlined herein redundant: Lucy Blue, Okasha el-Daly, Martyn Gregory, Emad Khalil, Geoffrey King, Duncan Lees, Jim Mower, and Geoffrey Tassie. I am also grateful to Tania Tribe who made many comments on the manuscript (any errors, of course, remain my own responsibility), and as usual Peter Kemmis Betty at Tempus has been a paragon of patience whilst the book changed shape over the last three years. Finally I dedicate this book to my favourite travelling companions: Sarah (who took so many of the photographs presented here) and little Thomas, and also respectfully to the memory of Nora.

Niall Finneran
London and Alexandria
Easter 2005

BIBLIOGRAPHIC NOTE

Key references are cited in endnotes rather than in Harvard form. I have had to be somewhat sparing in the extensive use of references, and have only cited those works of direct relevance to the present work and moreover which should be easily accessible to any scholar or interested layperson. The following abbreviations are used:

BSAA: *Bulletin de la Société Archéologique d'Alexandrie*
BSAC: *Bulletin de la Société Archéologique Copte*
CE: *Coptic Encyclopedia* (A. Atiya ed. (1991); eight volumes (New York: Macmillan))
JEA: *Journal of Egyptian Archaeology*

INTRODUCTION

SPACE, PLACE AND IDENTITY

> Alexandria must have been a city comparable to New York, the two ruling
> elements being in the first place Greek and Jewish and in the second British
> (or Irish) and Jewish. And just as New York is a dazzling symbol of the New
> World, so was Alexandria of the Hellenistic culture.[1]

The Egyptian city of Alexandria has historically suffered from something
of an identity crisis, never sure of its position either geographically or
culturally as an essentially Egyptian and *African* city, or looking towards
southern Europe as part of the Mediterranean social and economic system. This schizophrenia has manifested itself in a rich and varied cultural
amalgam, provoking imaginative metaphors such as those offered in
the quotation at the top of this chapter. This sense of dual identity – in
fact, as will become clear, we may even speak of many identities – has
helped create a legend, a mythology of Alexandria, created and nurtured
over 2000 years. This schizophrenia is also mirrored in the debates surrounding the context of Egyptological studies as a whole: how is the
Egyptian cultural achievement as a whole viewed? Historically Egypt
has been seen as part of the western Asian or Mediterranean system, yet
it seems to be forgotten that physically, culturally and emotionally Egypt
belongs squarely to Africa.[2] Alexandria is effectively an African city, albeit

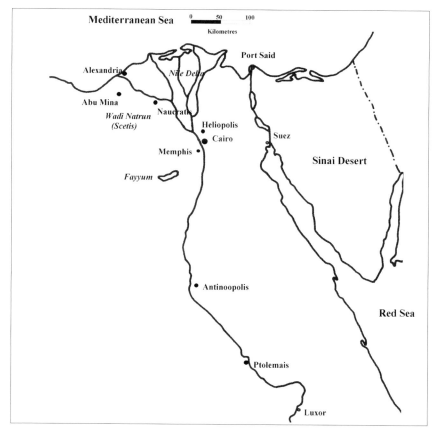

1 Location of Alexandria in the Western Nile Delta in relation to other key Ptolemaic/
late Antique cities of Egypt, and major modern cities

with a strong European flavour and many other competing cultural
sub-strands.

Alexandria's cosmopolitan identity has deep roots and has left us a
rich legacy. Just consider some of the historical associations conjured up
by the city: its very existence is witness to the triumph of one of history's
greatest generals, Alexander the Great; the city is a byword for Hellenistic
glory, the interface where the European, Greek world met that of the far
older African, Egyptian civilisation, resulting in a flowering of science,
art and literature; the stage upon which the final glories of the ancient
Egyptian pharaohs were played out under the shadow of the conquering
Romans; a diverse and highly cosmopolitan trading port of late antiquity,
dominating eastern Mediterranean trade yet also an important centre for

the development of early Christian thought and philosophy; and then, after the Arab conquest of Egypt, a rapidly declining star only reinventing itself as a town of sensuous delights and rich literary association in the late nineteenth century. And then what? Alexandria today, with a magnificent new library recalling its ancient glories of learning and wisdom – and as modern Egypt's second city – is a charming if occasionally down-at-heel summer holiday resort, consciously playing on its past, yet retaining a capacity for self-reinvention. It is this ability to shift identities that makes Alexandria, as an urban and cultural phenomenon, such an intriguing city.

The complete cultural history of Alexandria (or archaeology of the city) has not been written, and will probably never be written. Like so many other books written about the city the present work cannot claim to represent the total picture. More detailed and often period-specific works tackle this vast tapestry in a more coherent and compartmentalised manner. This book sets out to be a generalised and long-term historical narrative, but with reference to a major archaeological theme: the idea that although apparently physical urban space remains unchanged, the symbolic associations within those spaces evolve and shift. This concept requires more explanation. When teaching an advanced undergraduate course at the School of Oriental and African Studies in London over the period 2000-5, I tried to convey the impression that the history of Alexandria represents a fine example of cultural and spatial *syncretism*. The idea of syncretism is often applied to elements of material culture and put simply means the ability of culture to absorb elements of other, alien cultures. It is often used to refer to Christian material culture, where, for example in the case of early Egyptian Christianity the ancient, pharaonic ankh symbol (a looped cross) is quite easily absorbed into the Christian milieu, although the fundamental meaning of the symbol is different in both contexts. The religion of voodoo is a text-book case of religious syncretism, a meeting of Roman Catholic belief and African traditional religion and from a modern, western perspective, so-called New Age religions are regarded as being syncretic in character because they are made up of so many different ideological threads, Wicca, native American, Buddhist ideas *inter alia*.

To recognise the idea of syncretism demands that we do not operate within strictly defined boundaries; meanings of material culture are fluid. I would argue that we can extend the argument and make the same case for meanings in space: this is what I term spatial syncretism. Simply stated, and by way of an example connected explicitly with the present book, how often do we find in relation to sacred sites in late antiquity the construction of churches on top of pagan sanctuaries? There are many other examples of reuse of sacred space: the Umayyad Mosque in Damascus, Syria, for instance occupies the space of a Christian church which in turn was situated within a Roman temple. Perhaps even earlier Semitic inhabitants of the city used the place as a sacred locus. Who knows how many meanings, for instance, are embedded in the politically and ideologically charged space of the Temple Mount in Jerusalem? Alexandria is a syncretic space because it initially combines the Greek and Egyptian cultures, and then successively absorbs Jewish, eastern Semitic, Roman, Christian and Islamic belief systems. As a cosmopolitan city it would have been impossible for syncretic motifs *not* to be present. It is this theme that makes the city such an interesting archaeological case study, arguably a more diverse entity than many other ancient towns.

In relation to the problem of trying to translate these ideas in a teaching environment, I was not able to recommend a work that could give an overall narrative of these altered meanings in place and space within Alexandria over a period of almost 2500 years. The unusual nature of the chronological boundaries of the course I was teaching (north-eastern Africa from 330 BC to the present day) made it difficult to identify a single source book. I have therefore tried to write a book to tackle the long-term picture, a resource designed to introduce the biography of a very important city and give coverage to areas that have been hitherto ignored, yet one that will hopefully be accessible to the interested student or layperson. I hope to highlight some fascinating areas of the past and present of Alexandria that do not feature in the ordinary guide or other academic works on the city. The writing of this book also links in with the implementation of an archaeological project with which I am involved, a project that looks to map, using new survey technology, the sub-surface remains of the ancient city. This book then is a starting point, and I would hope, paradoxically, that the biography of the city presented here will be rendered obsolete by future research. But this is to anticipate matters and it is worth emphasising again that this can only be a general narrative. There are more academic and literary works about the city that address more specific issues than I could cover here. It is important to mention a number of core works that have informed my approach to this book, given impetus to it and have emphasised the problematic nature of the primary sources with which we will be dealing. In this connection, it would be worthwhile recalling a very apposite quote from one of the most important works on late antique Alexandrian history:

> The modern study of Alexandria has fallen into the cracks between the disciplines of ancient history and papyrology.[3]

This observation was made in connection with the concept of the academic/literary approach of the 'urban biography' of the late antique city; whereas many of these great cities of the eastern Mediterranean world of late antiquity (and it is to this period-specific, post-Classical world that we refer here), Alexandria – although obviously important – had been rather left behind, neither inhabiting the intellectual realm of the Egyptologist nor of the ancient historian. Reconstructing the biography of this city cannot be solely a project for archaeology alone; there are too many methodological problems associated with this approach, too many small pieces of the jigsaw to fit together. We need to utilise a more wide-ranging perspective. A number of important works published over the last 40 or so years have already begun to set the foundations for the scholarly study of this most important city.

Christopher Haas' wide-ranging and detailed work (see note 3 above) – itself a period-specific book – has filled this gap admirably, neither emphasising a wholly narrative nor wholly thematic approach. This important book brings to life the perception of ideology and space and socio-economic developments within the late antique city at time of general social, economic and political uncertainty across the Roman world, when Germanic tribes stood poised along the Rhine frontiers, in the east the Persians threatened and above all when Christianity was becoming a powerful social and ideological force. Haas shows how these uncertainties translated to the urban landscape of Alexandria. Remaining with the period-specific approach to Alexandria's history, we should also recognise Peter Fraser's compendious study of Alexandria under the Ptolemaic dynasty;[4] Fraser's masterful work remains important and as a guide to the nascent cosmopolitan entity of Alexandria in the first three centuries BC has never been bettered. At the other end of the chronological spectrum a recent French series of workshop and conference papers has focused on Alexandria in medieval times, from the late Byzantine period onwards. In archaeological terms these are uncharted and potentially rewarding areas of study.[5]

These three core works essentially provide an important scholarly resource upon which we can begin to build a long-term urban biography, as well as a starting point for understanding how Alexandria as a city functioned over three different time periods and under three markedly different political and social regimes. But, as if to echo Haas' comment above, these studies (certainly in the case of Fraser) emphasise the gulf between the papyrological and the 'ancient-historical' approach. There remains, however, another key and often overlooked literary source that will prove its worth to the scholar of Alexandria well into the future. This source is neither 'academic' – in the strictest sense of the word – nor is it particularly 'state-of-art', yet as an invocation of the place and its spirit it remains important. E.M. Forster's *Alexandria: A History and Guide* [6] was first published in 1922 in Alexandria, and was written during Forster's service there during the First World War. The book itself – a classic of travel literature – took a long time to gain popular following; many copies of the first (1922) edition were lost in a fire at the publisher's warehouse[7] and a second edition was only published in Alexandria as late as 1938. The 1961 US and UK editions – reprints of the first Alexandrian edition of 1922 – have proved to be exceptionally popular, an enduring legacy of a cosmopolitan city now long disappeared and in the words of Lawrence Durrell, a resident and chronicler of Alexandria in the middle years of the twentieth century, both a testament to a master of literature and a memory of 'a phantom city which underlay the quotidian one'.[8] There are many other historical sources that will be encountered during this narrative and those discussed above are personal choices for accessible and thorough introductions to different periods of Alexandria's history, but what of the physical, archaeological evidence of the past? What biases and sources govern the creation of this picture?

As Haas recognises,[9] the archaeological evidence for reconstructing Alexandria's past is decidedly thin; such is the density and antiquity of settlement in a relatively small area, much has been destroyed over the years, or lies deep and inaccessible. The pace of development of the city has resulted in much destruction of important archaeological deposits. A detailed recent work by the French archaeologist Jean-Yves Empereur, the most important modern archaeological scholar of Alexandria,[10] presents the extensive fruits of mainly rescue-led (i.e. salvage) archaeological excavation under his direction there over the last 20 or so years. It is only by sheer chance that new archaeological sites are identified, and being salvage archaeological sites often have to be investigated more quickly and in far less detail than the archaeologist would normally desire. The archaeologist is really held at the whim of the developer or builder and the recognition and investigation of sites is therefore entirely piecemeal and fortuitous (although Empereur's excellent work has shown the possibilities afforded by maritime archaeological investigation, beyond the reach of developers and a strategy peculiarly suited to Alexandria, where a number of important coastal sites have been inundated over the years by the sea). In summary, then, although much valuable archaeological work has been undertaken – and here one must also make mention of the extensive Polish research excavations at Kom el-Dikka in the centre of the city (*colour plate 4*) – the data yielded by modern *scientific* excavation are relatively sparse, and in many cases publication of sites excavated before the Second World War is not satisfactory. The urban biography of Alexandria cannot be written neither from a wholly archaeological perspective – which represents an incomplete and biased picture – and nor can it be written from a wholly text-based approach which again relies upon selective sources. Any study of the cultural history of Alexandria should look to broad horizons and utilise a range of methodological approaches.

But there is so much more to the myth of Alexandria. The bare bones revealed by archaeological excavation, papyrology or ancient history represent a small part of a wider and more diverse picture. This book is not a work of ancient history, archaeology or art history alone; as I emphasise above, it tries to draw on a number of sources and looks at the long-term narrative. In order to make sense of the wider picture, the longer narrative thread, we need to contextualise the data within a 'traditional', narrative framework using a chronological rather than thematic approach as articulated by Haas. A brief overview of the structure of this book will clarify how this problem is approached, although an obvious weakness is apparent in the somewhat arbitrary nature of the boundaries of the chapters and their names.

In chapter one a very broad synthesis of the history of Alexandria from its foundation up to the present day is presented, emphasising the context of the city within the wider Egyptian framework and considering in part the major socio-economic and cultural shifts that have played a part in shaping the identity of the place. The city itself is also physically contextualised within its broader landscape; essentially taking an east–west journey through the city and its environs we reflect upon the diversity and range of historical associations embodied in the city and myth of Alexandria and a number of chronological vignettes are presented that emphasise the idea of syncretism of space and cultural cosmopolitanism.

From the historical and geographical context presented in chapter one, we move to the core of the book: a consideration of how continuity and change in the religious life of the city is reflected in the story of Alexandrian culture. Essentially chapter two deals with the 'pagan' city (a definition which we shall see is not entirely satisfactory). We will consider Alexandria as a centre for Hellenistic, native Egyptian and subsequently Roman religious belief. Here we have in microcosm a flavour of our longer narrative; we will investigate the impact of Hellenism upon the life of the city and try to deduce just how much native Egyptian culture was subsumed into this new syncretic belief system, how Alexandria became a seat of 'pagan' learning, how the effects of Hellenistic, Alexandrian scholarship were subsequently felt down the centuries and from this cosmopolitan perspective try to assess the impact of religious change under the Romans. In addition we will consider the emergence of Alexandria as an outward-looking, cosmopolitan city – a theme that continues to the present day – and more specifically we tackle the thorny and difficult issue of trying to define and recognise specific ethnic and social identities on the basis of physical evidence.

Already this idea of an Alexandrian cultural identity, or sense of schizophrenia is building up, especially from the perspective of layering of religious belief – just how 'Egyptian' is the city, or is it merely a European, Mediterranean urban space transplanted to an African context? In chapter three the picture becomes even more complex. Here we will deal with the construction of a Christian identity, we will meet dynamic 'pagan' thinkers and vigorous Christian theologians who made Alexandria one of the most important intellectual centres of early Christianity and whose relationship rapidly declined to violence and forced seizure of sacred spaces. An interesting theme in this connection is why some places were respected and retained their original identity and why others were subjected to change in role. Again one must consider how this vibrancy and mix of religious belief is reflected at the socio-economic and cultural level. Can we speak of a Jewish perception of Alexandrian space, or even a Christian one? But we must go further still in our narrative, because for the greatest part of its existence as a city Alexandria has been neither pagan, Jewish nor Christian: it has been predominantly Muslim. Perhaps more than anywhere else Alexandria represents an idealised picture of how three major related world religions have co-existed in some form of harmony.

In the final chapter we complete the story of Alexandria and its important place within global religious history, and assess the cultural impact on the city of the coming of Islam in the seventh century. There are also a number of other themes that one must touch upon here, especially in relation to the construction of a definition of Alexandria as a Muslim city – and importantly in the context of the relative decline of the city's importance. There are other variables at work in the long-term narrative. Virtually all the important political players of recent western history have challenged for the domination of Alexandria: Turks, French, British, German and Italian. How has the memory of conflict altered and affected our picture of socio-cultural religious syncretism? And in this regard we should consider too the impact of this Muslim Alexandria – a new definition and a new identity, a cyclic reinvention – upon the western artistic mind. How has this cosmopolitan background shaped the way in which the idea of Alexandria has been packaged for both western and Islamic popular cultural consumption?

In summary it is hoped that this book adequately conveys something of the sense of adaptability, adventure, eclecticism and socio-cultural dynamism inherent within the narrative of Alexandria's rich history. It will show something of the multi-vocality of meanings and symbols growing out of the topography of the city itself and will consider how a legend and mythology has been created and nurtured. It is important today that the story of a vibrant, dynamic – and above all cosmopolitan – *eastern* city through the ages should be heard. Alexandria's most important legacy is religious and ethnic tolerance, an ideal that is unfortunately topically very apposite today in the current climate of the region. So this is Alexandria, the city and myth: a place physically rooted in the east, looking outwards, accepting ideas and peoples, fostering an atmosphere of relatively peaceful co-existence (for most of its history) of the three great related world religions. Alexandria and its history represent the best of Egypt, ancient and modern; this history speaks of flexibility, intellectual enquiry, enjoyment and above all an atmosphere (for the most part) of religious acceptance. This is a lesson that would be well learned elsewhere in the world today.[11]

one

SITUATING ALEXANDRIA: HISTORICAL, GEOGRAPHICAL AND THEORETICAL CONTEXTS

Modern Alexandria has long outgrown its ancient historical confines. The city that the visitor sees today is far removed from the planted Hellenistic version of the fourth century BC. More than any other Egyptian city Alexandria has evolved and changed, this is a story of flux and urban evolution almost without parallel in Africa. Our narrative of the history of Alexandria – and the shifting socio-economic and ideological perceptions of that urban space over time – has an easily defined starting point: a foundation that has been described extensively in historical literature, a story that has been repeated across the centuries. The story of Alexandria is perhaps best understood at the outset with some reference to the context of the modern city and its surroundings and in this chapter we will look at how many layers of the past can be 'excavated' from the present. Before considering the present urban topography we need to consider the broader and general historical context surrounding Alexandria's growth and development, a narrative which essentially mirrors the social, cultural and economic history of Egypt from the late fourth century BC to the present day. The following section presents an outline of the major historical reference points within the story of the city of Alexandria; the second section of this chapter looks at the modern topography of the city and presents a geographical context to the present study.

SETTING THE STAGE: HISTORICAL CONTEXTS

In this section we will look at the major turning points in the history of Alexandria with special reference to the wider historical situation in Egypt from around the beginning of the Ptolemaic period at the end of the fourth century BC. At this juncture, very generalised socio-historical themes will be introduced: dates, places and personalities. More detailed and specific themes will be discussed within the relevant chapters. The most obvious starting point for this broad survey is a brief consideration of how Alexandria came to be established, and this naturally involves a consideration of the personality and role of that charismatic historical figure Alexander the Great (356-23 BC), an individual whose exploits have recently been rediscovered by a global audience and whose conquests still have considerable geopolitical resonance today.

Within the long history of the classical world and the story of Greece there is surely no more powerful personality than Alexander III of Macedon, better known as Alexander the Great. We know much of this man's great deeds; many sources – such as Plutarch's biography, as well as the works of Arrian, Strabo and Polybius – provide an overview of his heroic life, yet essentially there is no new source material, either archaeological or epigraphic, that casts new light on his story and his personality.[1] Alexander's enduring legacy – especially important in the context of the present study – was the ideal of a cultural pan-Hellenism in the ancient world, not just a military conquest and economic exploitation of new lands, but also an extension of Greek culture into the east. This meant that Greek ideas, philosophy and religion were imported into the conquered regions. Yet this was not a one-way dynamic; equally important was the notion that useful cultural elements from outside the Hellenistic sphere could be happily incorporated into Hellenistic cultural life. Alexander's was at one time both a *political* and *cultural* empire; he believed in syncretic values and he could almost have been an orientalist, in the old-fashioned sense of the word (by this I mean that he took a great pleasure in the aesthetic values of the 'Orient').[2] Where he took on political roles of kingship in Babylonia and Egypt, he was careful to observe and embrace the ideological rituals that went with the secular status of the king.[3] This observance of kingly ritual also undoubtedly had useful political connotations; it offered a way of exploiting latent goodwill among the newly conquered peoples and tapped into a shared social memory. The Anglo-Indian *Raj*, for instance, used great traditional ceremonial in this way to link the exploits of the Mughal rulers with those of the British.

Alexander was born into the royal family of Macedonia (roughly in the area of modern northern Greece, not to be confused with the modern state of that name, a former Yugoslavian republic) in 356 BC at a time of great Greek and Persian rivalry.[4] He was the right man at the right time for Greece; in 334 BC he assumed the kingship of Macedonia and rode southwards to Corinth to renew the Hellenistic pact that bound the disparate Greek states together. Now was the time to settle the Persian problem in the east. Persia under the Achaemenids had been a regional power since the time of Cyrus II (559-30 BC),[5] and under Cambyses II (529-22) defeated the armies of the Egyptian pharaoh Psametik III – the last pharaoh of the 26th (Saitic) dynasty – at the battle of the Pelusiac mouth of the Nile in 525 BC. The Persians thus became masters of Egypt as well as most of western Asia. Alexander sought to make a decisive military move against the Persians and in doing so created a legend as a brilliant military tactician and general.

In 334 the Greeks landed at Troy and subjugated the Achaemenids in Asia Minor, defeating the armies of Darius III at the battle of the Granicus River. Alexander moved southwards, to Egypt, where he overthrew the Achaemenid satrap Mazaces and captured the capital city of Memphis.[6] Alexander's stay in Egypt was brief; in keeping with his cosmopolitan, syncretic outlook, he sacrificed to the Egyptian gods at Memphis and continued northwards into the Delta. Pausing at Lake Mareotis, he decided upon a place to build his eponymous city – to be his burial place – before continuing onwards to consult the oracle of Amun at the desert oasis of Siwa. Alexander had briefly marked out the overall plan of his new city before leaving, but he never saw its completion. There was still unfinished business in the east.

In 331 Alexander struck at Mesopotamia, capturing Babylon and then continuing eastwards pursued Darius and his broken armies past Persepolis into Bactria, where they were finally brought to heel. The defeat of the Achaemenids resulted in the subjugation of a vast region stretching from the shores of the Mediterranean to the Himalayas and saw the spread of Greek culture and language as far as what is modern Afghanistan. An important central theme is apparent in the mechanisms of the conquest and the ideology behind it. Alexander, whilst promoting the ideals of panhellenism – bringing the light of Greek culture to the east – was not averse to borrowing local customs and elements of ideology. In a true syncretic dynamic, Alexander absorbed – out of respect and intellectual curiosity and as we have seen political acumen and expediency – a range of different ideological concepts. When Alexander was enthroned as Pharaoh at Memphis, in the Temple of Ptah, he sacrificed to Apis and engaged in the active repair of Egyptian religious buildings that had fallen to ruin. This behaviour was in stark contrast to that of the Persian king Xerxes, whose defilement of the Apis cultic centre made him bitterly hated in Egypt. At coronation ceremonies in Babylon and in Persia, Alexander similarly reinterpreted the ritual of making the sacred king, basing the ceremony in local tradition, yet also making innovative changes to the ritual that clearly reflected his Greek heritage.[7]

In summary Alexander's philosophy was based upon the ideal of a superior Greek culture, allied to military excellence, yet he also recognised and respected the beliefs and traditions of the conquered peoples – in a word he was a multi-culturalist, albeit within certain limits.[8] Alexander also had a mythical idea of his own antecedents within the Egyptian royal pantheon. This thread of continuity, a holy genealogy, was based on his belief that his father should be identified with Nectanebo II, Egypt's last native born 'Egyptian' pharaoh/king.[9] Yet the very speed and effectiveness of this rapid cultural and military conquest proved to be its own downfall; when Alexander died at Babylon on 10 June 323 BC, his legacy – shaped by the force of his personality – was stamped across the entire region, yet this 'Empire' lacked an integrated bureaucratic state machinery. It was a case of too much, too soon; there was no clear succession mechanism in place. Upon Alexander's death the Empire was divided among his most able generals. Egypt fell under the influence and administrative satrapy of Ptolemy, who as Ptolemy I (Soter) began the true development of Alexandria as an urban centre – incidentally, one of at least 17 such cities to bear the name in the Hellenistic world – and who crucially kept alive the spirit of Alexander's syncretic outlook.

In the words of E.M. Forster, 'the average Ptolemy is soft; he has the artistic temperament but no passionate love of art'.[10] This is unfair; in essence the Ptolemaic dynasty which ruled Egypt until its incorporation into the Roman Empire in 30 BC kept alive the ghosts of pharaonic Egypt, yet added a vigorous Greek intellectual steel. It was under Ptolemy I Soter (meaning saviour) that Alexandria developed as an important urban centre and flourished as a city of trade, politics and learning during the reigns of the early Ptolemaic kings. Ptolemy himself was originally a companion of Alexander's from Macedonia, Greek in upbringing and temperament, but upon Alexander's death he assumed the bureaucratic title of satrap of Egypt and essentially became an old-style Egyptian pharaoh, carrying on the vision of his illustrious predecessor. As Alexander's other generals proclaimed themselves kings of their satrapies and progressively abandoned Alexander's central philosophy, so Ptolemy followed suit and in 304 finally announced himself king of Egypt, and thus became the founder of the Ptolemaic dynasty (see Table 1, below).[11]

TABLE I: THE PTOLEMAIC DYNASTY 304 BC–30 BC

Ptolemy I (Soter)	304–285 BC
Ptolemy II (Philadelphus)	285–246
Ptolemy III (Euergetes)	246–222
Ptolemy IV (Philopator)	222–205
Ptolemy V (Theos Epiphanes)	205–180
Ptolemy VI (Philometor)	181–145
Ptolemy VII (Neos Philometor)	145 (murdered as a child)
Ptolemy VIII (Euergetes)	145–116
Ptolemy IX (Soter II)	116–80
Ptolemy X (Alexander I)	106–88 (co-ruler)
Ptolemy XI (Alexander II)	80
Ptolemy XII (Neos Dionysus Auletes)	80–51
Ptolemy XIII	48 (co-ruler)
Ptolemy XIV	47–43 (co-ruler)
Ptolemy XV (Caesarion)	43–30 (co-ruler)
Kleopatra VII	51–30

Ptolemy I had been an able general and he realised that he needed to be on his guard against the manoeuvrings of his former comrades. Through his acquisition of lands in Arabia, the Levant and Cyprus he was able to create buffer zones to forestall any attacks on Egypt. His son Ptolemy II is principally remembered for his interest in developing Alexandria as a cultural centre; it was under Ptolemy II that according to legend 72 rabbis were gathered upon the Island of Pharos to complete a Greek translation of the Hebrew Bible (known as the Septuagint),[12] and he was also responsible for cultivating a relationship with the nascent Roman Republic, one that would ultimately last almost 1000 years. Ptolemy III is known for his extensive military conquests to the west in Cyrenaica (modern Libya), to the south in Nubia (northern Sudan) and to the east in the Levant; under him the Ptolemaic Empire was at its zenith. When in 217 BC Antiochus III of Syria attacked Ptolemaic possessions in the Levant, the Egyptian army under Ptolemy IV defeated him soundly at the battle of Rafah on the Sinai, but disaffection was brewing at home. Famine, high taxes and resentment of their Greek overlords were causing trouble amongst the Egyptian peasantry who started a chain of revolts against the centre of Ptolemaic power at Alexandria. During the reign of Ptolemy V, we find the introduction of one of the most resonant names in Egyptian history; Kleopatra I – daughter of the defeated Syrian king Antiochus III – was the first in a long line of consorts and regents who held the Ptolemaic Empire together over the next 200 or so years.

Essentially the theme of the later Ptolemaic period is one of gradual shifting towards the newly powerful orbit of Rome and an erosion of the overseas power base, allied to extensive intrigue within the royal court at Alexandria. Continued Syrian Seleucid political and military pressure also told, and all the while emissaries of Rome were working their way into the political system of Ptolemaic Egypt which was becoming more corrupt and dissolute. The Roman writer Diodorus Siculus (writing in Book XXXVII of his *History*)[13] reports on the visit of Scipio Aemilianus Africanus to Alexandria at around 136 BC. At this time Ptolemy VIII (who ruled Egypt alongside his wife and sister Kleopatra II and his other wife, her daughter, i.e. his niece-wife, Kleopatra III) was a grotesque, fat caricature of a ruler and to Scipio's disappointment the renowned mouseion of Alexandria was devoid of scholars. Alexandria clearly did not make a great impression upon him and over the next 80 years the Ptolemaic system began to break down still further, reflecting a decline in the cultural and economic fortunes of the city itself.

The reign of Ptolemy XII signalled the beginning of the end. Nicknamed Auletes (the piper), he was a weak monarch who fled to Rome in 58 BC, leaving the throne in the care of his wife Kleopatra VI Tryphaena and daughter Berenice IV. Auletes was restored to the throne through Roman pressure and on his death in 51 BC his daughter

Kleopatra VII became the last in a line of independent Egyptian kings and queens stretching back over four millennia. The end of the Ptolemaic Empire and the beginning of Roman domination marked the end of an independent Egypt, arguably until the Fatimid period. Kleopatra had actually concluded marriages with her younger brothers, Ptolemy XIII (killed 48 BC) and Ptolemy XIV (47-44 BC), although her greatest affections were reserved for Julius Caesar, who had ruthlessly pursued his rival Pompey across the eastern Mediterranean. Kleopatra bore Caesar a son, Caesarion, and after Caesar's assassination in 44 BC she returned to Egypt to rule again. In 37 BC, Kleopatra married Mark Antony (with whom she had twins Alexander Helios and Kleopatra Syene and another son, Ptolemy Philadelphus) although inevitably their political desires brought them into conflict with Caesar's nephew Octavian. The ensuing war resulted in defeat at the Battle of Actium in 31 BC and the deaths of Mark Antony, Kleopatra and Caesarion ushered in the beginnings of direct Roman rule over Egypt.[14]

Under Octavian (Caesar Augustus), Egypt became an integral part of the Roman Empire. Economically Egypt was important for its agricultural productivity and it became a favourite country for the Emperors. Augustus and his successors saw themselves – like Alexander – as heirs to the pharaonic legacy. Primary political power within the country, however, was vested in the Prefect at Alexandria who was able to rely on the support of two Roman legions as garrison troops (there were about 5000 men per legion); beneath him lay the system of 30 *nomoi* (administrative districts) that had been instituted by the Ptolemies for local governance and were based upon earlier pharaonic land divisions. Unlike the Ptolemies, who had maintained separate judicial systems for Greeks and native Egyptians, Roman justice was open to all, but some measure of Egyptian independence remained such as the use of the old calendar and minting of coins.

Perhaps the most important socio-cultural event during the first 200 years of Roman domination was the emergence of Christianity as a major religion. The Christian belief found a ready breeding ground in Alexandria in the first century AD; its proximity to Palestine and the relatively large cosmopolitan Jewish population there provided ideal conditions for the faith to develop (although Egyptian Coptic tradition emphasises an Apostolic origin, tracing the emergence of Christianity in Egypt to the ministries of St Mark in the AD 40s). Persecutions by the

Roman rulers were particularly hostile and widespread: Nero's in AD 64, Aurelius's in 161-80, Severus's in 193-211, Decius's in 249-51, Valerian's in 253-60 and finally those of Diocletian from 303-5 (the latter particularly savage in Egypt and enshrined in Coptic folk memory, so much so that the Copts reckon their calendar from the date of Diocletian's accession in 284). All these episodes deepened the sense of unease in what was now perhaps the most Christianised region in the Roman world.

The Edict of Milan issued by Emperor Constantine in 313 removed the official threat to Christianity and Alexandria became the power base of the Egyptian Christian Church, a role it retains to this day, although the Papal residence is in Cairo. Doctrinal disputes in the first 400 years AD affected the unity of the Church, none more so than those that engendered the schism after the Council of Chalcedon in AD 451, where the Egyptian church – with its belief in the single nature of Christ, human and divine inseparable (miaphysis) – broke away from the Byzantine 'orthodoxy' alongside sizeable numbers of Christians in Syria, the Caucasus and Ethiopia. Politically Egypt remained within the Byzantine (eastern Roman Empire) world (the Empire had been formally divided after the death of Theodosius I in AD 395) and although many Egyptian Christians adhered to the pro-Chalcedonian, Byzantine Orthodox line, the anti-Chalcedonian, miaphysite movement was gaining strength, particularly in rural areas in the shadow of an extensive and dynamic monastic system.

As on the wider Roman/Byzantine stage, the fifth century was a time when external pressures began to make themselves felt on Egypt. In the south, Nubian pastoralist groups such as the Blemmyes raided the southern borders of Egypt, and from the east the Persian armies of Chosroes invaded in 616, ending Byzantine political domination of Egypt, if only briefly. In 629 the Byzantine armies had recaptured Egypt, but far beyond Egypt's borders a new religious force was gathering. In the deserts of Arabia in 632 the Prophet Mohammed had died and now from that quarter came large armies of Arabs who had adopted his new and dynamic faith: Islam. The Arab armies pushed westwards and in 636 defeated the Byzantine armies at Yarmuk (modern Syria). The way to Egypt was now open.

In the fourth century BC, Alexander the Great had essentially created a Graeco-Egyptian syncretic religion, the coming of the Romans saw again an adaptation and mixing of two belief systems, whilst the emergence of Christianity in Egypt was based upon a Palestinian, Judaic inheritance. The advent of Islam changed the face of Egypt forever. Islam was born amongst the Arab tribes of the Hejaz in north-western Arabia, fostered by the charismatic Prophet Mohammed. Mohammed's successors – Khalifs – were charged with spreading the word among the Arab populations in Arabia and in the near east. The political background was propitious; the Christian Byzantine and Zoroastrian Persian Empires squared up against each other across the near east and almost unnoticed the forces of Islam infiltrated the region. After the Arab victory at Yarmuk, a force of Arabs attacked Byzantine Egypt under the capable leadership of their general 'Amr ibn al-'As. In 640 the Byzantine forces were routed at the Battle of Heliopolis; the former Roman garrison centre at Babylon-in-Egypt (in modern Cairo) fell in 641 and finally in September 642 Alexandria herself surrendered after a siege; 'Amr noted that he had taken command of a city of '4000 baths, 400 theatres and 40,000 Jews'. Egypt would henceforth be primarily an Islamic country (Table 2).[15]

TABLE 2: ISLAMIC EGYPT PERIODISATION (AD)

Umayyad governors	641-750
Abbasid governors	750-868
Tulunid dynasty	868-904
Ikshidids	935-969
Fatimids	969-1171
Ayyubids	1168-1250
Mamluks	1252-1517
Ottoman control	1517-1805

From the outset, Egypt had swapped membership of one empire for that of another, although the Arab 'empire' was clearly less politically integrated than the Byzantine version and was obviously more ideological in character. Given an often vicious history of Christian factional infighting, the predominantly Egyptian, miaphysite (i.e. anti-Chalcedonian) Coptic Christians had welcomed the end of Byzantine rule and the triumph of Islam – the hated pro-Chalcedonian, Orthodox 'Melkite' Byzantinists were now out of power and their influence waned accordingly, although an Orthodox Patriarch remained in the city (and indeed does to this day). It is too simplistic, perhaps, to speak of Arab favouritism to the Copts, but it is clear that the Melkite links to the old order did count against them. 'Amr essentially made a fresh start, although to some degree the Byzantine state machinery remained relatively intact; it had to be retained to enable him to rule effectively over his vast new acquisition. The new capital – sited at the strategically important apex of the Delta – was founded near the Roman garrison at Babylon-in-Egypt. Named Al-Fustat (meaning 'tent' and reflecting its camp-like nature), the capital would shift again during the Fatimid period to a nearby spot which would be named Al-Qahira (meaning triumphant). These new Islamic capitals soon coalesced into a single large metropolis: Cairo. The triumph of the Arab armies signalled the decline of Alexandria as a major political centre, although it retained – as headquarters of the Patriarchates of the Orthodox and Coptic Churches – a key spiritual importance and as the most important entrepôt to Egypt maintained an extensive economic significance.

The Umayyads – a dynastic family based at Damascus in what is modern Syria – gave way to the Abbasids in AD 749, and the political focus of the Arab empire switched further to the east with the foundation of a new capital at Baghdad. In 868 the Abbasid governor of Egypt – Ibn Tulun – threw off Abbasid political control and sought a more independent path. The experiment was short-lived and soon Egypt was back under Baghdad's direct rule. In 935 the governor of Egypt Mohammed Ibn Tughj tried to repeat Tulun's actions, but the Ikshidid dynasty – and the political independence of Egypt – was again a brief episode. Under the Fatimids Egypt truly became an independent state, tearing away the last links with the Khalifs of Baghdad when in 969, under the command of the general Gohar al-Siqilli al-Rumi,[16] Egypt was secured for the Fatimid dynasty.

The early Fatimid period is characterised by a succession of external threats to Egypt. In Palestine, Seljuk Turks were in control and in 1055 had taken the capital of the now weakened Abbasids at Baghdad. They now threatened Egypt directly – even more so given that fact that unlike the Shi'ite Fatimids, the Seljuks were Sunni Muslims.[17] The establishment of powerful Latin Kingdoms in the Levant after the First Crusade of 1095 threatened the Muslim domination of the region and when the Crusaders attacked Egypt in 1168 differences between Sunni Seljuks and Shi'ite Fatimids were forgotten and the two joined forces to defeat European ambitions in Egypt.

During the late twelfth century, the nephew of the Khalif of Baghdad began to carve a name for himself as a capable soldier, general and above all an enlightened leader. Salah ad-Din (1137-93) proclaimed himself Sultan of Egypt and Syria, guaranteeing Sunni domination in the region and founding the Ayyubid dynasty in 1168. This period is marked in the earlier centuries by continual pressure by Crusader armies who were finally defeated in the late thirteenth century. During this time Ayyubid power was waning considerably and a new political force was gaining power within the ranks of the Sultan's very own army in Egypt. Mamluks were Turkic/Caucasian slave soldiers who were much prized for their bravery, loyalty and superb horsemanship. Large corps of Mamluks formed an elite within the Egyptian armies and in 1254, in response to perceived injustices from their master, they installed a soldier of the Bahriyya corps, Ibagh, as Sultan upon their assassination of the last Ayyubid Sultan Turanshah. Under the command of the famed soldier and Sultan Beybars, the Mamluk armies dealt with the remnants of Crusader power in the Levant and moved decisively against the Mongols threatening Syria during the mid-thirteenth century. The capture of Constantinople in 1453 and the triumph of the Ottoman Turks over Byzantium had repercussions for Egypt; in 1517 they moved against a weak Mamluk army in Syria and took Egypt.

Essentially the Ottoman Turks ruled Egypt as a vassal state, but the size and extent of their possessions weakened their political coherence and the Empire was often prone to attack. In 1798 Napoleon, seeking to move against British strategic interests in India, invaded Egypt. Cut off from the sea after the naval defeat by Nelson at the Battle of Abu Kir bay near Alexandria, he set up a quasi-French protectorate introducing radical socio-cultural reforms. It is from this period that the compendious and still highly useful survey the *Description de l'Égypte* dates. In 1801 a combined British and Turkish force ousted the French and upon the British withdrawal in 1803 Egypt reverted to Ottoman control of a sort, although this time nationalist sentiment in Egypt had been aroused – as indeed had European interest.

The development of Egyptian nationalist awareness is attributed to Mohammed Ali, an Ottoman governor of Egypt (Pasha) from 1807 to 1849; he severed the links with the Mamluk beys and introduced a more independent style of leadership. In 1882 a disaffected army officer called Orabi led a revolt against Ottoman rule and European involvement in

Egyptian affairs; this revolt provoked the British naval bombardment of Alexandria and the final defeat of the rebels at the Battle of Tel el-Kebir at the hands of the British Army. Britain was now the occupying power and although executive power remained in Ottoman hands, it was the British who essentially controlled politically and economically all of Egypt. After the First World War – when Egypt played a decisive role in the defeat of the Ottoman Turkish armies of the near east – the country was offered a degree of self-determination guaranteed by the treaty of 1922 which established King Fuad as the first native *Egyptian* monarch since the Fatimid period.

Nationalist sentiment, orchestrated by the Wafd party under Sa'ad Zaghloul (for whom one of Alexandria's largest squares was named) kept up the pressure for reform, but the beginning of the Second World War stifled the movement as the British needed to secure the strategic situation of Egypt against neighbouring Axis pressure. As in World War One Egypt played a key role in the Allied victory; the Axis advance through Egypt – which would have cut through to the key oilfields of the near east – was checked at El Alamein in 1942. After the war pressure grew for a fully independent Egypt, with no British troops stationed on its soil. The abdication of the last king, Farouk, at Alexandria on the 18 June 1953 saw the establishment of a Socialist republic under General Gamal Abdel Nasser. The post-war period was marked by conflict with Israel, and then, under President Sadat a move towards peace, and the Egypt of today under President Hosni Mubarak is one of the wealthiest and most stable countries in Africa. Let us now turn to a consideration of the modern face of Alexandria and try to understand how the historical narrative outlined above has impacted upon the city and its region.

SETTING THE STAGE: SPATIAL CONTEXTS

> Once the first sense of estrangement is over, the mind finds its surcease in the discovery of the dream-city Alexandria which underpins, underlays, the rather commonplace little Mediterranean seaport which it seems, to the uninitiated, to be.[18]

Viewed from the air modern Alexandria does not exactly present a picture of Hellenistic glory as envisaged by its illustrious founder. The modern

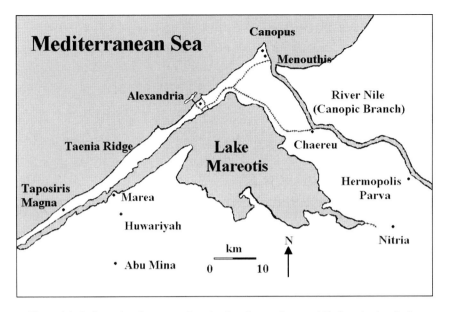

2 Alexandria in its regional context showing key late antique and Ptolemaic sites in its vicinity. In modern times Lake Mareotis has shrunk considerably

city of about four million people straggles almost 20km (12.5 miles) along the Mediterranean coastline to the west of the Nile Delta, but never reaches more than about 10 kilometres (c.6 miles) into the Delta hinterland. In terms of general geographical context, the city proper essentially covers the stretch of coastline from modern Abu Kir in the east to a point roughly in the area of the industrialised suburbs of El Max and El Dikheila in the west, although delineating these modern urban boundaries is not easy. Southwards, is the traditional boundary of the city, the northern shore of Lake Mareotis (in Arabic Bahra Maryut). In ancient times this was a vast expanse of fresh water providing all manner of resources for the ancient city and was the centre of a region with a very distinctive culture of its own. The original lake was bounded on the east by the now-silted Canopic branch of the Nile which separated it from another lake to the east, Lake Edku (south of modern Abu Kir); it was thus well connected to the inland waterways of the Delta and the Nile itself. The wines grown here were celebrated in Rome, and such was the agricultural productivity that three major cities – Plinthine and Taposiris Magna on the northern shore, and Philoxentite on the southern shore – flourished here. Now the 'Lake' is divided into two roughly equal-sized, rather polluted lakes with the new town of Medinet el Amirya el Guedida at its south-westernmost corner. Mudflats and industrial sprawl encroach upon the lake, now a sad remnant of its former self, yet in places one might luckily encounter bitterns or moorhen on the rich green margins of the saltpans. The conurbation, through new suburbs, industrial areas and coastal holiday resorts seems almost to creep westwards, reaching out in the distance along the axis of the railway and coastal road (Route 55) towards Hannoville, Abu Sir and El Alamein.

The modern urban boundaries are entirely elastic; combined demands of burgeoning population, fuelled by rural immigration, industry and tourism – Egyptian nationals tend to be the prime customers for the new coastal resorts along the road westwards – govern Alexandria's growth potential.[19] Alexandria, the urban centre and its economy, does not exist in isolation, although physically it may seem like the last north-western outpost of urban life in Egypt. Caught between the physical antitheses of the fertile Delta and the barren Western Desert, Alexandria has always adapted socially and economically, and now as the second largest city in Egypt shows no sign of losing this adaptability and capacity for reinvention.

That Alexandria does not exist in isolation is an obvious point, perhaps, but one that is often overlooked by archaeologists and historians; the wider context is part of the story of Alexandria as an urban entity, the relationship and dynamic between city and country. Here I will attempt to delineate some of the most important topographical zones with an eye to their relevance in the broader story. We will move on an east–west axis through the city and its immediate landscape, imagining, say, an approach from the Nile Delta at Rosetta, as if we are moving from the core agricultural area of ancient Egypt – the 'sown' – westwards into the desert through Alexandria itself. In former times, the approach and arrival to the city from Europe would be directly by sea, into the harbour; the modern traveller (perhaps using the train) arrives at Masr station in downtown Alexandria, having experienced a view on the way in of intensive agricultural and industrial works and recent, rather drab suburban architecture. Neither of these approaches is satisfactory in terms of seeing the wider historical context. Our symbolic approach to the place does not follow the traditional routes, but views the city as unfolding gradually, both physically and historically in a series of topographical vignettes, discrete places with a story to tell, embodying the rich heritage of the narrative outlined in the first section of the chapter.

1 The modern Christian cemeteries at Shallalat reflect Alexandria's syncretic heritage; here Coptic tombs surround an attempt at a classically-proportioned tomb façade, which itself houses the front of an abandoned car. *Sarah Finneran*

2 The modern library recalls Alexandria's reputation for scholarship in the ancient world. *Sarah Finneran*

3 The different alphabets on the sweeping external wall of the new library of Alexandria emphasises its internationalist perspective, a legacy of the Ptolemies. *Sarah Finneran*

4 Kom el-Dikka, or the mound of rubble. This site, to the north of the railway station, and near the city centre has been the focus of Polish archaeological activity, and excavation here has yielded a great amount of information about the late antique city. *Geoffrey Tassie*

5 The bell tower of the modern Coptic Cathedral of St Mark rises among the nearby tenement buildings, modern skyscrapers and minarets. Lawrence Durrell did not regard its architecture highly, but it is a dignified building in the modern Coptic style, the domes on the roof recalling an older form of Egyptian monastic architecture. *Sarah Finneran*

6 The Mursi mosque, much remodelled but a dramatic addition to the waterline of modern Alexandria. *Sarah Finneran*

7 The Mamluk fort of Qaitbey, built upon the foundations of the fabled lighthouse on the Island of Pharos. *Sarah Finneran*

8 The archaeology of the recent past. Skeletons of a modern war scar the deserts to the west of Alexandria; here maritime archaeologists, working away from Ptolemaic statuary around the Pharos, have recovered the remains of an RAF Spitfire from the seabed. *Sarah Finneran*

9 The so-called Alabaster tomb, possibly Ptolemaic in date, and located in one of the western, modern cemeteries (the Latin, Roman Catholic cemetery) has been suggested as being a candidate for Alexander the Great's tomb. *Geoffrey Tassie*

МАРКОС

اذكر يارب عبدك

د. أسعد خليل   د. سالم أسعد خليل   د. سمير حلمى أسعد

Above: 10 The Chatby necropolis in the eastern–central portion of the modern city; an ancient place of rest now encompassed by busy roads. *Geoffrey Tassie*

Left: 11 A modern mosaic of the Apostle of Egypt, St Mark, in the Coptic Cathedral of St Mark, Alexandria. The iconography of the Pharos lighthouse is highly symbolic in the Christian context. *Geoffrey Tassie*

12 A wall painting of Athanasius in the Church of St Antony, in the Monastery of St Antony in the Red Sea region of Egypt. Athanasius was one of the key figures in early Christian Alexandria and a dynamic theologian. *Niall Finneran*

Right: 13 The interior of the Greek Orthodox Church of St Sabas. The old monastery was demolished in 1970, and the present church structure, notable for its fine iconostasis, dates from 1975, although the structure does incorporate earlier elements. Note particularly the ancient pillars here, which may have been reused from the original church. *Geoffrey Tassie*

Below: 14 Sunset over the Corniche and the still waters of the eastern harbour. *Lucy Blue*

Abu Kir (see 3; located to the east of the ancient city of Canopus) marks the beginning of this journey, although historically and physically there is little to recommend this place, now a thriving fishing port. The site of the naval action between Nelson's British and Napoleon's French fleets in 1798, Abu Kir marks the easternmost extremity of the Alexandrian coastline. Moving westwards we arrive at Canopus, or more accurately the site of Canopus. Canopus represents, through our traverse of the landscape, some of earliest first evidence for the interface between the pharaonic Egyptians and the Greeks and therefore evidence of an essentially schizophrenic perception of urban order, not quite pharaonic, not quite Greek. Until the Canopic branch of the Nile silted up and Alexandria took over as the major entrepôt on this coast, Canopus was a large and exceptionally important city which gained something of a reputation in Roman times as a hedonist's paradise full of earthly delights. Canopus was just one of four cities that dominated this coastline before the construction of Alexandria (the others being Heraklion, Menouthis and Thonias). Greek mythology suggests that the city was named after Canopus, the helmsman of the Greek King Menelaus, who was killed by a viper bite and was buried in the area, but it is more likely that the name derives from a deity – possibly associated with Osiris – named Canup.

We know much about the city from such classical sources as Herodotus (c.450 BC), Seneca (first century AD) and the geographer Strabo (c.63 BC – AD 21); built as a link to the inland Greek settlement at Naucratis,[20] continual problems with the silting up of the Canopic mouth of the Nile and the growth of Alexandria put paid to its key role (although it did form part of an inland freshwater canal link, alongside Heraklion and Menouthis, with Alexandria). Apart from acquiring a reputation as a somewhat seedy holiday resort in Roman times, Canopus – and her sister cities – formed an important part of the western Delta economic system in late antiquity. This wealth was reflected in extensive public buildings, chief among them being the Temple of Serapis of which fragments of the granite slab called the *Naos of the Decades* survive in the Museum at Alexandria and the Louvre, Paris. But nothing remains of Canopus on land. Textual sources suggest that the city was destroyed as late as the eighth century AD and recent geoarchaeological and maritime archaeology work in the environs of Abu Kir Bay has thrown some light on its fate. It appears that a disastrous series of Nile floods around AD 741 saturated the landscape around the cities; the ground then liquefied and the cities physically slipped into the sea.²¹ Recent underwater archaeology work by a French–Egyptian team led by Franck Goddio has located a large number of monumental remains in three separate areas on the bed of Abu Kir Bay at a depth of about ten metres (30ft) and these sites would seem to accord with the positions of Canopus, Menouthis and Heraklion, and have yielded many small finds including Arab coins of a mid-eighth-century date. As we will see with Alexandria, it is probable that the sea itself hides more archaeological secrets than the land.

Continuing a sweep westwards, along the slightly indented coastline now lined by modern building developments, we find more historical surprises. Just as the site of Canopus embodies ideas of cultural syncretism and cosmopolitanism, so does the nineteenth-century former royal palace at Montazah. Set in a vast lush green park on a headland, the palace was built on the orders of Khedive Abbas II in 1892 and it displays an eclectic architectural mix of Ottoman and Florentine influence, a real east meets west style – like the city itself. Its current role is as a closed-off, presidential guesthouse, although the grounds are open to the public (somewhat incongruously the place is overlooked by a Sheraton hotel). We continue our survey along the main east–west coastal road, grandly named *Tariq Gamal Abdel Nasser*. Toponyms in Alexandria (as well as Egypt and many other Arab countries) reflect the persistence of memory and the power of tradition. Gamal Abdel Nasser was born in Alexandria at a time when European and Egyptian lived in some sort of cosmopolitan harmony (1918), although the relationship was admittedly one-sided, and it is tempting to suggest that the prevalent socio-cultural mores of post-First World War Alexandria may have had an effect on the young man who went on to a great career as an Arab statesman. Along this road we meet the full sweep of Alexandria's history; westwards from the beaches of Sidi Bishr, through the colonial-period suburbs and modern seaside developments, we catch our first glimpse of the Hellenistic layer of Alexandria's past: at the necropolis of Chatby we may view third-century BC rock-cut tombs, evidence of the Hellenistic-Ptolemaic symbolic view of the afterlife, a city for the dead positioned outside the city walls. The tombs (now sadly flooded) were built in the shape of a Greek house, or *oikos*. Juxtaposed with the Hellenistic-Egyptian view of the afterlife are the modern multi-faith cemeteries at Shallalat nearby. A confusing and arresting array of Roman Catholic, Protestant, Greek Orthodox, Coptic, Maronite, Armenian and even Jewish headstones present themselves;

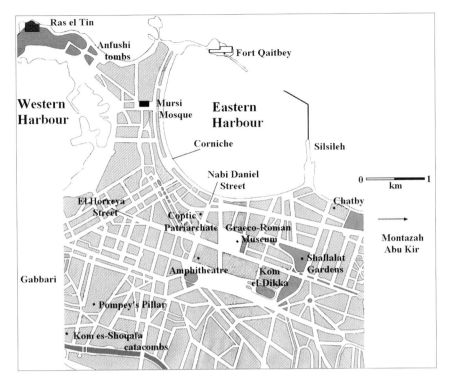

3 Map of the central area of the modern city showing key roads and sites

this is a city of the dead, reflecting the cosmopolitan past: a complex network of paths and alleys among extravagant family vaults, graves and funerary chapels; on the headstones one sees a multitude of alphabets and languages, and faded black-and-white photographs of dignitaries and ordinary people, scarcely less impressive than the necropolis elsewhere in Alexandria and witness to the cultural variety and cosmopolitan outlook that permeates the fabric of the city (*colour plate 1*).

This is also an area rich in scholarly association. Alexandria's wealthy Christian past is commemorated in St Mark's College, an establishment now part of the University of Alexandria and open to all, Christian and Muslim alike. At the edge of the water we find the latest incarnation of the Library of Alexandria, a witness to the powerful imagery conjured up by the past and the association of Alexandria with global scholarship rather than the 'little Mediterranean seaport' of Durrell. According to its mission statement,[22] the library is designed as an international resource, a scientific, academic and cultural repository. The foundation was formally inaugurated by the signing of the Aswan declaration on 12 February 1990 by – among others – President Mubarak and Queen Noor of Jordan and was partly funded by the United Nations Education, Scientific and Cultural Organisation (UNESCO). Built on the seafront at the eastern edge of the Eastern Harbour (according to scholars near to the site of the Brucheion, the Palace quarter), the building – designed by the Norwegian architects Snohetta and begun in 1995 – presents an imposing aspect (*colour plate 2*). It is not just the choice of the site of the library, with its immense historical associations, that recalls images of the past. The design is symbolic; a circular shape recalls the geometry studied in the original foundation; inclined towards the sea and surrounded by a moat of water, the shape is akin to the Egyptian Sun, emphasising enlightenment and scholarly illumination. The surrounding wall of the moat – built of smooth Aswan granite – is decorated with a variety of world alphabets, symbolically echoing the cosmopolitan nature of the original foundation (*colour plate 3*). As a cultural resource the library's proposed scope and future plans are ambitious; there is room for over four million volumes, to include manuscripts, microfilm and other media, and over 500 staff are expected to work there upon its final completion.

This library represents a huge financial investment. Its design – and in fact its very *raison d'être* – recalls Alexandria's cosmopolitan Hellenistic and pharaonic past; it is almost as if Alexandria the city has rediscovered a golden age, a corporate identity, when it was at the centre of the Mediterranean's cultural life. As such the metaphors and symbolism inherent in the conception and execution of this new building are profound; the library is an indication of a strong folk memory, a living past. The journalist Hala Halim, writing in the Egyptian *Al Ahram* weekly, drew attention to this phenomenon of building a romanticised past;[23] she noted a very overt Hellenistic revivalism going on, with the appearance of noticeably Hellenistic-style statues on traffic roundabouts. The inhabitants of Alexandria seemed, at the time of the opening of the library, to be sold on the Hellenistic motifs, yet, she noted, were seemingly ignorant of their pharaonic heritage. In other words, like the physical aspect of the city, the inhabitants were beginning to look outwards again, their attention focused upon the horizons of the Mediterranean rather than the pharaonic heritage of the narrow river confines behind. They unconsciously reinvented their social memory.

Continuing westwards from the new library building, we have

reached, in essence, the historic heart of Alexandria, but there is little left that bears witness to Alexander's original urban conception. From Sa'ad Zaghloul square (*Midan Sa'ad Zaghloul*; another important Alexandrine toponym, recalling the hero of the Egyptian nationalists), we can view many layers of history in a compact central area. Here we would be standing upon the Caesareum of Roman times, where the Temple of Augustus stood (itself later an important early Christian cathedral), as well as the twin obelisks now known as 'Cleopatra's Needles' (which stand on London's Embankment and in New York's Central Park) – but now nothing of this once vast complex remains except what we may read of in ancient literature. Other ghosts of the past survive; the faded Art Deco glamour of the Cecil Hotel, once Alexandria's foremost society hotel, and the street alignment of *Sharia Nabi Daniel* – running southwards from the south-eastern corner of the square – probably preserves the original Hellenistic north–south route of the *Street of the Soma* (Hellenistic cities were planned along the shape of grids, this pattern has generally survived; see figs 3 and 11) where, according to tradition, the body of Alexander the Great is to be found under the crypt of the Mosque of Nabi Daniel.

The cosmopolitan nature of religious space is a common theme; within this area we may find a small synagogue that serves Alexandria's rapidly diminishing Jewish population and the stark white bulk of the recent Coptic Cathedral of St Mark (*colour plate 5*), reminding us that Alexandria, now predominantly a Muslim city, is still a Christian city. Just off this road we may find the Church of St Saba – itself built on the site of the pagan Temple of Apollo – that reminds us of a Greek Orthodox Christian cultural inheritance, and westwards, around Tahrir Square this syncretic Christian picture is completed by the Roman Catholic cathedral, the Anglican church of St Mark and the Maronite church. The Attarin Mosque is located here; again the economy and syncretism of spatial symbolism is evident, for here, according to tradition, was another place where Alexander the Great was buried and subsequently the site of a church built by Athanasius, one of the most dynamic figures in early church history.

The fulcrum of the ancient city, the crossroads of the north–south and east–west axes, may probably be identified with the intersection of *Sharia Nabi Daniel* and *Sharia Fouad/Horreya*. Somewhere beneath our feet here are the remains of the great *Mouseion*, the scholarly centre and library of

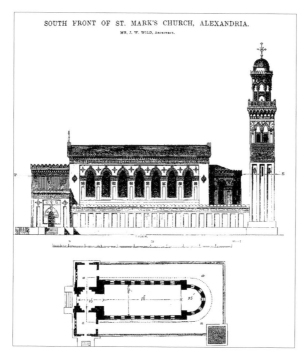

SOUTH FRONT OF ST. MARK'S CHURCH, ALEXANDRIA.
MR. J. W. WILD, Architect.

4 The Anglican Church
of St Mark which
although a place of
Protestant worship pays
homage architecturally to
the cosmopolitan history
of Alexandria. Reaction
to this hybrid building
when the plans were
unveiled in the 1840s was
not generally favourable.
The *Builder* noted that
its 'pointed architecture
sought to conciliate the
opinion of the Arab
inhabitants of Alexandria'.
From the Builder *5/9/1846*

international fame. This is a frustrating theme, always somewhere beneath
the feet are the ghosts of Alexandria – where are the tangible remains of
the classical city? The Graeco-Roman Museum founded in 1892 presents
some visible aspects of Alexandria's heritage, a heritage yielded almost
haphazardly by chance find rather than extensive scientific excavations.
Importantly for the context of our understanding of the past, a museum
of maritime archaeology has also been opened.[24] The foundation and
development of this museum clearly indicates where the future focus of
research-led rather than salvage archaeology in Alexandria will be. Near
to the railway station at Masr are the extensive Roman remains at Kom
el-Dikka (meaning, appropriately enough, mound of rubble) where many
years of excavation by a Polish/Egyptian team has uncovered a quarter of
the late antique city, complete with theatre, bath-houses, shops, roads and
houses dating from the fourth century AD.

In the south-west of the central area of Alexandria, in the suburb
now called Karmous, but an area which may accord with the much
earlier pre-Hellenistic Egyptian village of Rhakotis, Alexandria's classical heritage is visible again. Pompey's Pillar – a 25m-high (70ft) Aswan

5 The Graeco-Roman Museum in Alexandria. A nineteenth-century foundation that recognises the Cosmopolitan legacy of the city. *Geoffrey Tassie*

granite column – marks the probable location of the Temple of Serapis/ Serapeion, and the area is surrounded by subterranean chambers and cisterns. Confusingly enough – but appropriate for a city of blurred identities – this pillar has nothing to do with Pompey; it is a structure associated with the late third century and the Emperor Diocletian. Nearby, just up the hill, we find the extensive Roman catacomb complex at Kom es-Shoqafa, which dates from the second century AD and provides a tantalising hint as to what the once vast extra-mural Roman cemeteries of Alexandria may have looked like. These galleries remind the archaeologist of the possibilities of a fabulous chance find, for these extensive subterranean tombs (now endangered by rising ground water) were literally stumbled upon the last century when a local man and his donkey fell through a hole in the road into a burial chamber.

More than anywhere else the ghosts of Alexandria's past collect along the shore, the Mediterranean coast and harbour and the focus of international trade, along the line of 26th of July Street. More romantically and traditionally this is the *Corniche* of European invention (consider here the meanings and symbolism of Alexandria's toponyms; the shift-

6 Pompey's Pillar. Location of the famed Temple of Serapis. *Sarah Finneran*

ing names of roads and squares in response to new ideological and social identities) which encloses the eastern harbour. Here parts of Alexandria's past become more visible, and the ancient topography begins to make more sense. Along the road, we pass the large mosques of Terbana (originally built in 1685) and Abu al-Abbas al-Mursi (*colour plate 6*), which dates from 1943, although it was originally built by Algerians to commemorate a sixteenth-century Andalusian saint. We are now in the Anfushi residential quarter, formerly the Ottoman new town, and its presence bears witness to the way in which an urban landscape can physically change. In Ptolemaic and Roman times this was the site of the Heptastadion, a causeway linking the Island of the Pharos with the mainland, and dividing the eastern from the western harbour. Silt has gathered up along the old causeway and now Pharos is no longer an island, more a sinuous peninsula. This neck of land, heavily populated by teeming buildings, mosques and shops, was once largely under the waters of the eastern harbour and is the focus of the post-Arab conquest urban settlement. The modern curve of the *Corniche* bears little relation to the former coastline; prior to the silting of the Heptastadion the shore front pretty much ran in a straight line, and incorporated a number of smaller quays and harbour installations.

We continue around the sweep of the bay and find ourselves on one of the most important topographical features of the ancient world, although there is nothing to physically remind us of the fact. At the tip of the promontory, we find the fort of Qaitbey, a squat Mamluk building of late fifteenth-century date (*colour plate 7*), which although visually satisfying in its own right as a piece of Alexandrian heritage, lacks the visual scale and power of what used to stand there in ancient times: one of the seven wonders of the ancient world, the massive light-house. Of this – as with anything ancient in Alexandria, little remains – but out in the sea archaeologists have recovered large architectural blocks that may have belonged to the tower itself. It is perhaps to the seabed that we should look in the future for archaeological confirma-tion of Alexandria's past, such is the crowded nature of the landward Alexandrian present.

Here on the former island we may also find the fine Hellenistic-period limestone rock-cut tombs at Anfushi (Ras el Tin), and whose magnificent paintings evoke more than anything else the satisfying vis-ual qualities of the amalgam between ancient Egyptian and Classical arts. Also here is the expanse of the Ras el-Tin palace, another witness to the

7 Looking eastwards along the Corniche, the Alexandria of popular imagination. *Geoffrey Tassie*

power and pretensions of Egypt's recent royalty (the palace itself is probably sited upon the foundations of the Roman Temple of Neptune), and which saw the departure of Egypt's last king in 1953 for a life in exile. Also running westwards from the tip of the former island are a series of ancient breakwaters and harbour installations which may predate the construction of the main harbour works. Again, many pieces of the historical narrative crowd into a small geographical space, yet only ghosts remain. Imagine how this place would have looked 2000 years ago.

West of the island and past the western harbour – now a naval base – modern Alexandria resolves itself into a suburban sprawl of sorts. The road to the west, in the direction of Mersa Matrouh, follows the line of a distinctive topographical feature, the limestone Taenia (Abu Sir) ridge, which separates the freshwater lakes of Maryut from the sea itself. This is the historically important region of Mareotis to which we have already briefly alluded. Alexandria and the Mareotis region would have enjoyed an important symbiotic economic relationship in former times. Even as far back as the 27th 'Persian' dynasty of the mid-first millennium BC, Mareotis (also known as Marea) was a Nome (administrative unit) in its own right, bounded to the east by the Saitic Nome and to the south by the Nitriote Nome. The area belies its desertic appearance; it was the site of extensive monastic estates in the late antique period and was noted for its productivity, with an economy based upon fishing, papyrus, arboriculture, glass making and gypsum and nitre (sodium) extraction.[25] Its size was such (and its links to the Nile) that a freshwater port for Alexandria (Portus Mareotis) was built there in Roman times, but the hydrology of the area was always going to result in problems. By the twelfth century the lake had become a salty swamp, and in the nineteenth century the lake flooded with disastrous consequences at least twice, leading to a modern drainage and land reclamation programme which has entirely changed the character of the landscape.

Many strange historical anomalies and oddities are found in the seemingly inhospitable deserts west of Alexandria, all bearing witness to the imprint of time. The important site of Taposiris Magna, beneath modern Abu Sir, contained a fourth-century BC temple, which was converted into a Christian church in 391, during which time it replaced the important site of Marea as the Nomic capital. A small tower here (Burg el-Arab) seems to replicate the much larger lighthouse at Alexandria; it is in fact a tomb structure dating to the reign of Ptolemy II. At the modern monastery of Abu Mina are the remains of a fourth-century basilica of huge proportions, dedicated to the memory of the martyr St Menas, and in late antique times the site of a vast pilgrimage centre. Then onwards to El Alamein, the site of the battle in 1942 that effectively turned the tide of the Second World War; here in the dry desert air we may find at the museum a bewildering collection of machines of war from both sides (*colour plate 8*), contrasting with the neatly kept cemeteries and memorials for the dead of both sides. And one last historical oddity; the Marea area was the site of the fledgling United States' invasion of Egypt in 1805; at the behest of the US government, and in a bid to strangle piracy, a force of US marines and Bedouin landed here,[26] marking perhaps the beginning of the USA's global role.

This landscape, the place and space of Alexandria loosely defined, embodies a wide variety of historical experiences, from the pharaonic period to the still recent scars of the Second World War. Physically so much is invisible,[27] yet the ghosts remain. In this chapter we have intro-

8 Away from the disorder of the catacomb, a modern necropolis. Regimented and ordered within the landscape, the Commonwealth War Cemetery at El Alamein. *Sarah Finneran*

duced the historical and spatial contexts in general terms, setting the scene for the more detailed thematic, period-specific chapters that follow. We have seen too that it is hard to define both physically and spiritually where the city begins; this is equally true of trying to quantify its myth. How we perceive space is central to this study. The key theoretical thread that runs throughout this book, itself an attempt at a biography of an urban space, is the idea of understanding a syncretism of space, how meanings of place are layered, multivocal and never fixed. This is best illustrated with ideological space; why, for instance, the earliest Christians sought to appropriate sites that had immense pagan significance. We may also see similar ideas at work when we consider the impact of Hellenistic culture upon the fabric of the traditional and ordered pharaonic society; we must understand how the inhabitants of Alexandria re-ordered and re-conceptualised their habitual space in response to these profound social and ideological shifts. Alexandria, perhaps more than any other place in Egypt, best embodies this idea of shifting meanings in place and space over time. To sum up, it will become apparent that nothing in the biography of Alexandria's space is straightforward; meanings and symbols mount up, identities and boundaries merge, the narratives shift. One could even go so far as to argue that this, one of the ancient world's first manifestations of the cosmopolitan, multicultural city could be regarded as representing the postmodernist ideal; the fluidity of meaning, pastiche, diversity, a global village. Imagine it for a moment; a pre-modern, postmodernist city! No matter what theoretical perspectives we use, Alexandria always resists categorisation. It is this trait that makes it such an appealing subject of study.

two

EGYPTIAN SPACE, GREEK PLACE: THE 'PAGAN' CITY

THE GREEK AND EGYPTIAN WORLD: THE INTERFACE

The Greeks and Egyptians were always the dominant powers of the eastern Mediterranean world, and Alexander the Great's fateful encounter with Egypt and its culture was obviously not the first time that there had been a socio-cultural meeting between the Hellenic and Egyptian worlds. Small-scale economic and cultural interaction is known from as early as the Bronze Age, Aegean Mycenaean period (*c.* 1400-1200 BC); from the eighth century BC we find Egyptian bronze work on Crete and Samos,[1] and Herodotus mentions a Greek presence in Egypt as far back as the seventh century BC during the Egyptian 26th (Saitic) dynasty (663-525 BC). Greek mercenaries were also an important feature of the Egyptian military machine at this time, and it should also be noted that Ionian pirates ranged far and wide along the Mediterranean shores – another less formal and structured element of cultural contact between the two great eastern Mediterranean peoples.

The original site of the city of Alexandria was occupied by an Egyptian settlement (Strabo refers to it as being a city, although this is not clear)[2] called Rhakotis, but this may refer to the Egyptian name for the later city of Alexandria itself, and may derive from the Egyptian word *Raqa'ed* meaning 'building site' owing to the fact that the Egyptian workmen refused to recognise the new name 'Alexandria'[3] – an early statement of local resistance to the new Greek hegemony. Other records suggest that there may have been 16 Egyptian villages on the site of the future city, but without doubt Rhakotis must be regarded as being the largest and most important Egyptian settlement in the area, and some sources suggest that it served as a frontier post for the western Delta as early as the 18th dynasty (*c.*1500 BC).[4] It does appear that the Greeks already knew of the Island of Pharos – which would ultimately form a key part of the harbour complex and was the site of the famed lighthouse. Homer, for instance, in Book IV of the *Odyssey* tells of how Menelaus was becalmed off the Pharos Island when he returned from Troy and the name of a divine king of the Island (Proteus) is mentioned.[5] It is clear that the prospect of a safe anchorage and useful strategic situation as a possible entrepôt into the Nile and its lush and fertile Delta hinterland attracted the Hellenistic city planners. The geography of the area informed the ultimate design of the city; the Pharos Island lay offshore, and the coast-line itself formed a ribbon of land between the extensive Lake Mareotis behind to the west of the now-silted Canopic branch of the Nile.

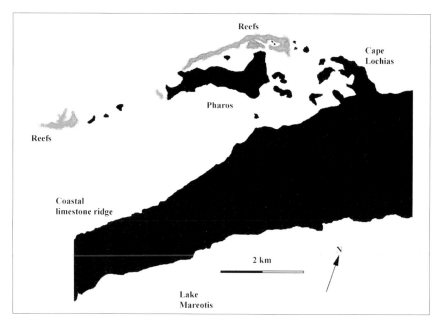

9   The original geomorphological situation of the city; the Egyptian settlement of Rhakotis was situated in what later became the southwestern corner of the Greek City on the northern shore of Lake Mareotis

From an economic and strategic perspective then this was an ideal site: excellent anchorages, a command of the inland waterways and access to an agriculturally rich hinterland. These were encouraging circumstances under which the planted urban entity could flourish, yet Alexandria was not the first Greek 'city' in Egypt; there are precedents for extensive Greek settlement in Egypt before the founding of Alexandria, and we may look to these as examples of how Greek conceptions of urban planning differed from the standard Egyptian model.

Before the foundation of Alexandria – this transplanted Hellenic urban space – the most important Greek settlement in Egypt was Naucratis on the east bank of the Canopic branch of the Nile, roughly adjacent to the modern village of El-Niqrash. Excavated by the noted Egyptologist Flinders Petrie, the town, which has been described by John Boardman as 'not like a colony…nor a simple trading post'[6] was centred around the Temple of Aphrodite in the south and the temple of Apollo Hera in the north – both edifices bearing witness to the ambition and wealth of its inhabitants and the centrality of the Greek ideological outlook. There was no room here for the sort of cosmopolitan perspective that became the theme of Alexandria's social and cultural life. This was a determinedly Greek space set in the Egyptian countryside, insulated and separated. The trade dynamic centred upon the town of Naucratis was not overly complex; Egyptians traded corn to the Greeks and the Greeks brought in luxury items – such as silver – to the Egyptian mercantile classes and aristocracy. Already taste for Greek culture was being fostered among the moneyed Egyptians; this was a very subtle form of economic colonialism, yet the relationship worked both ways, as exported Egyptian luxury items also found a ready market in the Greek world.

On a much smaller scale, the Naucratis settlement is mirrored elsewhere at Daphnae (Tell Defennah) on the eastern edge of the Delta. A seventh-century BC foundation, this settlement was the centre of the distribution of Corinthian and eastern Greek pottery throughout the Nile Valley;[7] again Greek luxuries were much sought after among the local Egyptian population. These cities were Greek in every sense of the word: socially, culturally and legally (it should be pointed out that within Hellenistic Egypt, only three 'Greek' cities were *legally* recognised: Alexandria, Naukratis and Ptolemais Hermaion in the Thebaïd) and they were obviously dominated by a Greek elite (a Priestly aristocratic caste oversaw the cultural and social life of these *poleis*), but the

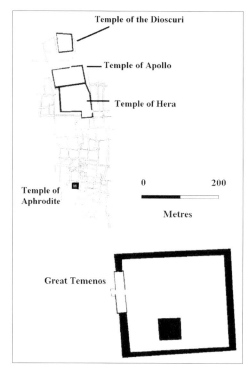

Temple of the Dioscuri

Temple of Apollo

Temple of Hera

Temple of Aphrodite

0   200

Metres

Great Temenos

10 Plan of the Greek city of Naucratis. Physically and ideologically the temples were at the centre of the urban space. Redrawn after W. Coulson (1996) *Ancient Naucratis Volume Two (The Survey at Naucratis and Environs Part One).* Oxford: Oxford University Press (figure 3)

majority of inhabitants – an urban underclass perhaps – were actually Egyptians.[8] The basic economic structure was focused overwhelmingly upon trade, with the exploitation of the local agricultural hinterland to support a luxury import and export trade.

In contrast to the idealised Greek city, built upon the generation of capital, and rigidly organised in a hierarchical manner, the Egyptian urban form was much freer and amorphous. The Egyptian concept of urbanism was much different from this transplanted Greek model; the early dynastic Egyptian model was to some extent a reflection of Mesopotamian urban space, but in Egypt the focus was very much upon the royal quarter. Egypt was a very stable society in comparison to Mesopotamia, and the accent here was upon the rural, a nested hierarchy of town and village rather than dominant and all-powerful city spaces.[9] Alexandria represented, for the first time, an attempt to bring rigid urban geometrical order to the Egyptian landscape; a linear grid pattern of streets internally organised into specific quarters and the whole enclosed by an external wall to delineate the urban world from the rural, the Greek from the Egyptian (or perhaps more elementally, in the eyes of the Greeks, culture from nature; this reflection of the perceived snobbery of the city dweller is something that is still reflected in our use of the word 'urbane').

Alexandria impacted upon the Egyptian landscape and psyche at many levels: economic, social, ideological and emotional too. It was more than just a new form of urban planning. The city was the focus of a wider economic and bureaucratic system within the landscape; returning to theoretical ideas of place and space, such a model would accord to a framework long used by archaeologists researching the phenomenon of complex societies particularly in the near east, a nested, hierarchical model suggested by Thiessen polygons, where we see a primary 'central place' surrounded by a rural and urban system of towns and villages which feed into the central marketplace, in terms both of materials and labour. This dynamic is referred to as being a symbiotic relationship in the sense that one part of the system could not exist without the other parts. In return for the wealth flow into the central place (the city) the flow outwards from the centre to the other units within the notional polygon would consist of redistributed wealth, political leadership and luxury goods.

We can apply this to the model of Alexandria and its hinterland; the Greek-style hierarchy of social space impacted upon the ancient organised landscape of Egypt (which, linked with pharaonic notions of 'urbanism', did not emphasise the primacy of the city at the centre of the social system). Alexandria here was the principle city, yet it was also an alien conception and in time it would not actually be recognised as being part of Egypt at all for, in the Roman period, the city would be called *Alexandria ad Aegyptum*, a term which implies a physical and legal separation;[10] it thus occupied a strange amorphous autonomous niche, a limbo, not quite Greek, not quite Egyptian. Hellenistic ordering of space outside of Alexandria in the rest of Egypt – the countryside or *Chora* – saw the pharaonic local government (*Nome*) structure largely retained and only slightly modified; the cities, *Metropoleis*, were the local administrative capitals of the retained regional *Nomes*, and beneath these cities, in a system of nested hierarchical units, were the villages that formed the framework of the agricultural base of Egyptian society.[11] Within the city itself, the fundamental administrative dichotomy was founded upon the people (*ecclesia*) and town council (*boule*). Greek-style democracy had permeated the Egyptian political landscape, but it is important to note that this democracy was not something that was open to all, and this factor ties in with the notion of ethnic identity within the city which we will consider shortly.

PLACE AND SPACE IN THE HELLENISTIC CITY

This new transplanted urban model of Alexandria was based upon the archetypal use of space within the Hellenistic city. According to tradition Alexandria, which was founded roughly upon the space of a pre-existing Egyptian settlement, was designed by the noted Rhodian architect Deinocrates and throughout the history of the city, a general economy of space is noted; successive conquerors' urban redevelopment and rebuildings never strayed too far from this zone, and often followed closely Deinocrates' original spatial model.[12] According to legend, the plan of the city was marked out by Alexander himself in grain; a flock of birds swooped down and carried away the grain outline of the city and this was regarded by all as a particularly favourable omen.[13] It is somewhat ironic that superstition played such a part in the founding of a city that would become renowned for strict scientific, rationalistic endeavour!

The main features of the new city space may be described thus (see figure 11). The primary east–west route, the Canopic Street, provided the major axis through the city; this route ran from the Canopic Gate in the east, to the Gate of the Moon in the west via the Gate of the Sun. This street, according to historical descriptions, was flanked by a porticoed walkway, and part of the route is preserved in the alignment of the modern *Sharia Horreya* (Horreya Street). In common with other Hellenic urban plans, this axis was crossed by a main north–south route; the Street of the Soma (so named because it passed by the tomb of Alexander, *Soma* is Greek for body) connected the harbour and palace area (around Cape Lochias) to the northern shore of Lake Mareotis at the southern edge of the city. This route would appear to roughly correspond to the modern *Sharia Nabi Daniel* alignment. The city roads were orientated in order to take advantage of the cooling summer Etesian winds that blew in from the sea and they would also have served as boundaries for the discrete residential quarters. These roads have been given a numbering system

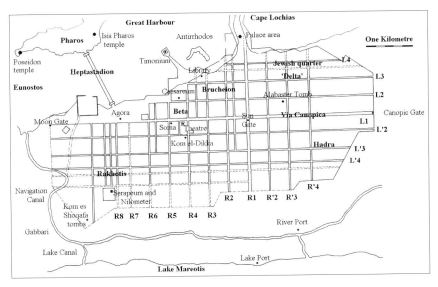

11 The key sites of the Ptolemaic and Roman city. The major temples and tomb complexes have been marked and the waterways through the city indicated. The codes of the streets are used in archaeological mapping of the city. The Polish excavations at Kom el-Dikka, for instance have revealed sections of Street R4. The Heptastadion which connected the Island of Pharos to the mainland silted over in the last two millennia

by archaeologists (shown on the conceptual maps used here throughout), and hypothetically, although they may be buried under centuries of accumulated debris, it should be possible on the basis of small-scale excavation to extrapolate their modern extents. For the most part their presence is to be detected in the alignments of the modern street plan which has retained a remarkably grid-like nature at odds with the rather haphazard development of the later Islamic city of Cairo.

At the physical and ideological centre of the new city was the tomb of the founder of the city, Alexander himself, although this is of course open to conjecture and no two legends agree on this. According to some traditions, Alexander had wanted his body to be thrown into the Euphrates – hoping perhaps that he could perpetuate the idea that that he would be joined again with the Egyptian God Amun who, after all, so he believed, had sired him.[14] It is possible that Ptolemy I took the body and moved it to Memphis, from where it was moved again by Ptolemy II to Alexandria, where it was placed within a communal royal tomb in the city; this action may be seen as a method of strengthening the ideological and political ancestry of the Ptolemaic dynasty and as a confirmation of the royal bloodline and ancestral rights to the city. This installation would be in itself a cultic centre, for Alexander was not just a political ruler; with the open and enlightened mind that characterised his personality he had enthusiastically absorbed the Egyptian notion of divine kingship, so he too was a God just as pharaohs had been in centuries past.

This tomb embodied in every way the means by which the Ptolemies viewed their place in the world, for here was a shrine – not a tomb – more a centre of a heroic cult. Heroic ideals played an important part in the Ptolemaic outlook, as is evidenced by the nature of their statuary which emphasises physical strength and power in the body. After the reign of Ptolemy II, kings were actually deified during life, and we find the development of a real syncretic ideal of Egyptian divine rulership and Greek hero cults.[15] Greek rulers were never accorded such elevated status, yet here in Alexandria we find the meeting point between heaven and earth, the political and divine worlds, the Greek warrior hero, the Egyptian divine inspiration. This tomb place embodied a number of meanings and to visit it meant a vicarious linkage with the great man himself. As with any famous building laden with meanings, a certain degree of mythology surrounds its exact whereabouts. Octavian, the future Emperor Augustus, claimed to have visited the tomb in 30 BC, and placed flowers there, and even later Arab sources claim that the body of Alexander could still be seen in the city in a tomb said to be on the site of the modern Nabi Daniel mosque. Another candidate for Alexander's tomb could be the so-called Alabaster tomb the Latin cemetery at the eastern edge of the town centre (*colour plate 9*). No other Hellenistic site in Alexandria has stirred so much controversy as the whereabouts of this tomb (if Alexander was indeed buried here at all and not elsewhere in Egypt or in his vast Empire). The quest for Alexander's tomb continues today, a testament to the power of the hero figure in modern popular imagination.

Apart from the high-status structures and temple precincts at the physical centre of the city, we need also to be aware of how the vast majority of the population was organised, something that archaeologists and historians have hitherto paid remarkably little attention to. A number of important contemporary historical accounts can tell us something of the daily life of the ordinary citizens. The administrative system of the Hellenic and later Roman city is described in detail by Philo,[16] who writes of five districts, each named after a letter of the Greek alphabet: Alpha, Beta, Gamma, Delta and Epsilon. The location of the suburbs of Beta and Delta (the latter held to be a Jewish quarter) are shown in *11*; the location of the others is conjectural. These quarters may be thought of as formalised suburbs, each with a special character. A Syriac document[17] dating to the time of the time of Michael Bar Elias, 'Jacobite' (Syrian Orthodox) Patriarch of Antioch, and drawing upon a first-century AD source, sets out a description of these quarters and it differs from the accounts set out by many other classical sources (such as Eusebius' *Chronikon*). This document gives the following statistics for each quarter (Table 3):

TABLE 3: THE QUARTERS OF THE ROMAN CITY ACCORDING TO A FIRST-CENTURY AD SYRIAC SOURCE

Quarter	A	B	Γ	Δ	E
Temples[18]	308	110	855	800	405
Courts	1655	1002	955	1120	1420
Houses	5058	5990	2140	5515	5593
Baths	108	145	?	118	?
Taverns	237	107	205	178	118
Porticoes	112	?	78	98	56

This is probably not an entirely accurate account of the city during the first century AD, for as the document itself makes clear, it has not taken certain areas of the city into account, such as the Serapeion, outlying settlements (such as Canopus and Nicopolis) and the Pharos, but a brief analysis yields some noteworthy statistics if we assume each 'quarter' to be equal in size. There are proportionally more temple structures in Gamma in relation to houses; this suggests that this quarter carried some ideological significance. In total there are over 21,000 houses, which is surely an underestimate, whilst the number of bath structures is consistent across three suburbs.

The whole city was bounded by a wall, about 15km (9 miles) in circumference. Gateways allowed for access at the western and eastern ends of Canopic Street and a number of canals were cut through the city itself. The wall could hardly have been an ideal defensive structure; in any case, the city itself (at least during the first centuries of its existence) could hardly be physically threatened. The purpose of this structure was to act as a clear boundary between city and country, but it was more than this. The wall surrounding Alexandria separated the predominantly Greek world from the elemental Egyptian countryside; already we are beginning to see the emergence of a dynamic that would become very important to the political organisation and allegiances of the early Christian communities; the dichotomy between *perceived* culture and nature, Greek and Egyptian. Again archaeology alone cannot throw light upon the way in which the walls and boundaries of the city were organised, we need to try to enter into a more imaginative reconstruction of spatial perception, and in any case the remains of the wall are highly fragmentary. A small portion of this wall is still visible in the Shallalat Gardens, abutted by a later Tulunid defensive tower; the quality of the masonry is excellent, although the walls were not strong enough to deter attacks by the Normans in 1153, 1155 and 1174. So much for a basic overview of the city on the land. Another key factor in the development and growth of the city, it need hardly be said, was its proximity to the sea and the Mediterranean trade routes, and it is to the sea and Alexandria's international outlook that we now turn.

12 Fragment of the city wall visible in the Shallalat Gardens. The tower dates from the Arab period, but incorporates granite column bases (possibly Roman) in its foundations. *Geoffrey Tassie*

CITY AND SEA: THE INTERNATIONAL DIMENSION

Alexandria obviously faces the sea, it is the entire *raison d'être* of the city. Alexandria looks outwards across the eastern Mediterranean, a place that receives, transmits, the place acts as a socio-cultural and economic 'middle man' at the junction between Egypt and the Mediterranean world. This area was always a place to set sail from, to reach out across the horizons to exploit new economic opportunities; it is no surprise that historically port cities have a character all their own, dwelling apart physically and emotionally from their hinterlands. But it is also important to recognise that although physical commodities flowed through the ports and quays, other more amorphous yet equally vital imported goods entered the city: ideas and ideologies.

According to the Palermo Stone inscription, it appears that the pharaoh Seneferu (the first king of the fourth dynasty, Old Kingdom (*fl.* 2613 BC)) built 60 ships to travel to the Levant (modern Lebanon) to secure supplies of cedar wood for his building purposes, and it has been suggested that this fleet must have set sail from a point somewhere near the mouth of the Canopic branch of the Nile at a place known as A-Ur, or the Great Door.[19] Although we have no explicit reference to earlier Egyptian use of the waters around what became Alexandria we do, it will be recalled, have evidence that the Greeks knew the value of the Pharos as an anchorage (Book IV of Homer's *Odyssey*). It has been suggested that there existed, at around the time of Homer's writing, a long eastwards breakwater extending from the Pharos; it is possible that this feature might be the earliest evidence for a harbour structure. If the tomb of Alexander and the temples and palaces became the ideological focus of the city, then the harbour became its economic life-blood and the conduit for the new ideas generated in the magnificent place of learning, the famed mouseion in the streets behind.

It was under the Ptolemies that the first major remodelling of the harbour itself occurred;[20] with an emphasis now on regional trade, effective anchorage and docking facilities were obviously important. Where Deinocrates brought linear order to the landscape, so the architects of the harbour progressively brought linear order to the sea-scape and coastline. Some of the most important structures in ancient Alexandria are associated with the harbour area, the primary zone of commerce. One of the key developments was the construction of a long dyke or

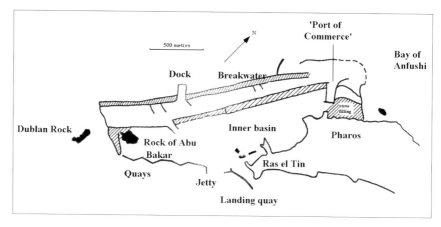

13 The oldest harbour works to the west of the Pharos Island. *Redrawn after L. Savile (1941) 'Ancient Harbours'* Antiquity *15: 209-232*

causeway connecting the Pharos island with the mainland thus form-ing two distinct harbours: to the east the *Megas Limen* 'great harbour' and to the west, beyond the urban boundary, the harbour of *Eunostos*, or the 'safe return'. Two entrances within the construction of the cause-way allowed for transit between the harbours. This 16-arch causeway was known as the *Heptastadion* (being seven *stades* in length, about 167m or 548ft), and over time, owing to tidal silting, this feature became the wide neck of land visible today leading up to the fortress of Qaitbey, its east-ern edge forming the northern portion of the modern Corniche, and subsequently the major focus of Islamic settlement in Alexandria.

Recent sub-surface, maritime archaeological survey in the eastern harbour has uncovered a number of small quays and bays on its eastern edge, and it is also clear that there are a number of man-made works on the north-western fringe of the Pharos Island too, but these structures cannot be dated with any great degree of accuracy. Given its proximity to the city, it was soon the eastern harbour and its quays that became the focus of maritime activity. This harbour enclosed an extensive area from the Pharos itself around to the easternmost point at Cape Lochias (mod-ern Silsileh) and it appears, from recent underwater archaeological work, that this harbour contained a smaller number of quays and harbours, one of which was probably a royal marina given its location adjacent to the royal palace.[21] A large slipway (there is a similar structure known from the quay at Corinth, Greece) known as a *Diolkos* was also located in this area.[22] It is certainly clear from ongoing archaeological research that the plan of the harbour is more complex than earlier surveys imagined and that there has been a large amount of building works there over time; indeed the coastline is still evolving, although the days of far-reaching international trade are long gone and the importance of the harbour at Alexandria has declined.

The most famous structure associated with the Ptolemaic harbour was the great lighthouse, the Pharos itself, one of the celebrated seven wonders of the ancient world. This was no simple structure to guide ships into the harbour; according to contemporary accounts, the beam of this lighthouse was visible from 160km (100 miles), indicating a major degree of complexity in the design of the lighting apparatus.[23] The tower itself was approximately 135m in height, and was designed by the noted architect Sostratos of Cnidus. Built within a colonnaded courtyard, the structure rose through four tiers, starting with a square tier, then an octagonal tier, cylindrical tier and finally a lantern structure; its weight would have been considerable, and it appears that there had to be an architectural reinforcement of the rock beneath to provide stable foundations which anyway would have been right on the edge of the solid rock.[24] Inside the main shaft were storerooms and lift arrangements to take the fuel (probably wood and naphtha) up to the main lantern. A 7m-high statue of Poseidon crowned the lantern and the whole edifice was faced in white limestone (some sources suggest marble, although any detailed description of the decoration of the Pharos is hypothetical);[25] in terms of sheer scale and colour it would have presented a very arresting sight, and its visual impact as a demonstration of economic power would have been considerable.

Frustratingly, as with many aspects of the archaeology of Alexandria's rich past, we cannot accurately visualise how this building looked. There are, of course, eyewitness accounts of the structure, and in a few cases roughly contemporary pictorial evidence; figure *14* shows a mosaic depiction of the Pharos – dating to around AD 539 – discovered at excavations at Gasr el-Libia, Cyrenaica (Libya) in 1957,[26] and another far-flung depiction of the Pharos was noted on a late Hellenistic Alexandrine glass beaker found at Bagram in modern Afghanistan.[27] Another important source for the appearance of this building is found in Roman-period coin motifs, which often show depictions of the most important city buildings;[28] coins showing the Pharos were minted over the reigns of six

14 Depiction of the statue crowning the Pharos from a mosaic in Gasr el-Libia, Cyrenaica (Libya). *Redrawn after R. Goodchild (1961) 'The Helios on the Pharos'* Antiquaries Journal *41: 218-223*

Emperors starting with Domitian (AD 81-96) and the building is either depicted alone or alongside a figure of the goddess associated with the island, *Isis Pharia*, whose statue crowned the structure.

What happened to the Pharos as Alexandria's fortunes declined is open to conjecture. In the Islamic period, the structure was reconstructed (although not to its earlier size) by the Tulunids during the period AD 868-905, thus indicating that there was still a considerable need for a lighthouse here. Although an earthquake in 956 severely weakened the Pharos, we do have eyewitness accounts that suggest it was still standing as late as the twelfth century, but another earthquake in 1303 destroyed the Pharos leaving only the first tier standing.[29] An artificial mound, known as the *Kom el-Nadura*, was constructed from the debris and it served as a rudimentary beacon structure and fort guarding the entrance of the eastern harbour, and then during the Mamluk period the site formed the foundations of the late-fifteenth century fortress of Qait Bey.

Over the last 40 or so years maritime archaeologists working on the seabed surrounding the site of the former Pharos have uncovered statuary that may have belonged to the Pharos complex itself, and there are other ghosts too. The distinctive tapered and tiered design of the lighthouse may have been copied by builders of the minaret of the late

RAViTMANS & SANS

15 A depiction of St Mark sailing into the harbour of Alexandria in the mid-first century
AD; from the Church of St Mark, Venice, Italy. *Sarah Finneran*

ninth-century Ibn Tulun mosque in Cairo (*17*); this may only be conjecture, as there are also clear parallels with the minaret of the Great Mosque
of Samarra (Iraq), but it is possible that the folk memory of the Pharos
still had a profound impact even in Islamic times. So many Hellenistic
symbols of power had this effect; they remained vital and played a key
part in the monumental creation of the urban space itself. This then was
the outward aspect of Alexandria's urban space, facing the sea, open to all
influences. If the sea was associated with being cosmopolitan, bringing in
economic wealth, people and ideas from the eastern Mediterranean, facing towards Greece, then the countryside was a different matter. Much
has been written about the city as an internationalist entity, but what of
the countryside surrounding it?

CITY AND COUNTRYSIDE: THE DOMESTIC DIMENSION

As one of the most important harbours in the Mediterranean Alexandria
was at the centre of the regional trade network, acting as a conduit for all
manner of goods, both luxury and domestic, to pass into Egypt and out
into the wider Mediterranean economy. During Ptolemaic times the

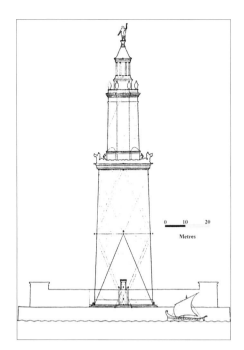

16 Above left: A proposed cross-section of the Pharos structure. Redrawn after M. Asin and M. Otero (1933) 'The Pharos of Alexandria: summary of an essay in Spanish by Don Miguel de Asin with architectural commentary by Don M. Lopez Otero. Communicated by the Duke of Alba, Corresponding Fellow' *Proceedings of the British Academy* 19: 277-292

17 Above right: The top of the minaret of the late-ninth-century Ibn Tulun mosque (Cairo) may reflect the original tiered construction of the actual Pharos itself, although a degree of Mesopotamian influence in its design must also be admitted. *Geoffrey Tassie*

city became an economic powerhouse; this much is evidenced from the design of the city and the use of monumentality. The Pharos, for instance, was at once a lighthouse, and a statement of power and wealth. Textual sources attest to the variety and amount of trade being handled through the city; one of the most unusual imports during the Ptolemaic period were monkeys, specifically macaques, who from the second century BC were shipped in from north-western Africa and transported onwards to the royal city of Memphis where they undoubtedly served a cultic role (many corpses of macaques have been found at the so-called baboon catacomb in Saqqara).[30] All forms of other luxury goods came and went: spices, ivory, wood, ceramics, metalwork, cloth and also *ideas*, for as we will see Alexandria was also a city of learning. But away from the excitement generated by a study of the truly exotic trade, we must be aware that the whole system was founded upon one very simple factor in the equation: the agricultural hinterland.

The hinterland of Alexandria was given over, economically, to intensive agriculture. Of particular importance was the Marea region, centred upon the margins of Lake Mareotis; this was an area where arboriculture, fishing and papyrus industries were important components of the local economy and it is important to recognise that the region also yielded extensive mineral deposits such as gypsum and sodium, making it a very rich landscape.[31] But the countryside is essentially a finite resource and the evidence for the detrimental effects of Alexandria's growing economic importance are clear to see; there is no doubt that over-intensification of agriculture in this region has had a marked effect on the landscape. There is only so much that can be taken out; the countryside needed careful management and on occasions the rural economy suffered from sheer overload. Water management is of special concern; a network of canals and ditches irrigated the areas around the city, but too much demand for water could result in a collapse of the system, and outbreaks of disease. This was a precarious balance, maintaining the commercial lifeblood of the city; this is best seen in the shrinkage of the once vast Lake Mareotis, which in early times was ringed by harbours and settlements, yet which became a salty swamp by Ottoman times (the sixteenth century).

Properly managed, this rural landscape could provide for the needs of Egypt's population, both rural and urban. Herodotus records that in the fifth century BC,[32] the diet of the Egyptians was overwhelmingly based upon bread (often made from emmer wheat; *Triticum dicoccum*), mixed vegetables and fish (dried or salted). Given a grain-based agricultural system, beer was the preferred drink of many classes of society, although the emphasis shifted in later Hellenistic times to viticulture, the drink of choice in the Mediterranean lands (beer is always regarded as being an 'African' drink).[33] Emphasis was placed upon maximising the available land for agriculture; the Delta itself was intensively farmed and settled, as were the river margins. Farming upon the nutrient-rich silt of the confines of the river banks was limited by the availability of the land itself and steps were taken to increase agricultural land by introducing advanced irrigation techniques; in Ptolemaic times, for instance, the Fayyum depression was intensively managed. Within this rich landscape no land could be wasted; oil crops (such as sesame, castor or linseed) were grown extensively on marginal and slightly saline lands where they thrived and provided a useful cash crop for the urban markets and flax formed a key resource for Egypt's growing textile industry. The fundamental base of the urban system of Alexandria was vested in the narrow river margins of the river and its tributaries rather than the long-distance exotic trade of the ships that came into the harbour past the mighty Pharos; the fields along the Nile nourished the artisans of the city and fed the brains of the philosophers.

The availability of a large and predictable agricultural surplus allowed the urban elites to support a dedicated cadre of artisans; this is something often overlooked when we consider the international orientation of Alexandria. During Ptolemaic times, for instance, the city was well known for its metalwork, glass, faience, papyrus and perfume industries. Distinctive Hadra pottery was made here; a fine clay, pale buff with black painted decoration which has been found all over the eastern Mediterranean. The extent of the luxury trade in the eastern Mediterranean and beyond, dominated by Alexandria, is witnessed by an anonymous mid-first-century AD work known as the *Periplus of the Erythraean Sea* which is essentially a guide to the trade networks and ports of the Red Sea zone; here the ships of Alexandria ranged as far as the Horn of Africa and came into contact, through the port of Adulis, with the Aksumite Empire of the Ethiopian highlands. It is clear that this extensive maritime trade network exploited not only the African interior for spices, ivory and other luxury goods, but Arabia too.[34] All this was made possible by the efforts of the Egyptian farmer, but we know little about him, in fact we know little about the day to day life of the consumers of Alexandria and its hinterland as a whole; epigraphic and archaeological interest tends to attach to the glamorous and therefore the elite.

During the first to third centuries AD detailed Roman census returns generally allow us to reconstruct the domestic economy of Egypt and Alexandria. Sadly, many of the (papyrus) census returns from Alexandria have not survived (the majority refer to the Arsinoite and Oxyrhynchite nomes in the south-west of the Delta, the rural hinterland of the city itself). At the beginning of the first century AD we have population estimates for the city of the order of 500,000 people;[35] as a whole, we see an intriguing population profile in which young males and widowed older women are represented in the census returns, something that might be a side effect of the organisation and recruitment for the Roman Army.[36] The make-up of the population suggests something that has been termed as being a 'high-pressure regime' where we see high fertility and high mortality rates reflecting a very typical Mediterranean 'domestic group organisation'.[37] At any rate, it is clear that Alexandria itself had a profound economic and social impact on its surrounding landscape; the Greek ideal of the city of high culture had changed the lifestyle of the indigenous Egyptian forever.

As befits an important economic centre, Alexandria issued its own coinage. The first Ptolemaic issues (which when instituted by Ptolemy I was essentially a closed coinage) were based upon the Athenian standard, and generally of silver with gold issues reduced considerably after about 270 BC,[38] showed an eagle on the reverse, and this motif survived the reform of the Imperial coinage under Diocletian in the fourth century.[39] The choice of motifs upon the coinage gives us some idea of the shifting ideological and political worlds within the city over time. Ptolemy's eagle and thunderbolt recalled a personal identification with the God Zeus, a definite statement of Greek divine power, and subsequent Ptolemaic kings, in common with the rest of the Hellenistic world, used the coinage to show their own personalities in the shape of coin portraits.[40] Latterly, and in common with the general theme of Alexandria's cosmopolitan artistic and ideological syncretism, Roman Imperial themes and Graeco-Egyptian motifs may be seen together on the coinage. The depiction of wheat ears on the coins (something that is incidentally also noted on Ethiopian Aksumite coinage of a later date) attests to the importance of the agricultural system and wider cereal trade; the issues of Antonius Pius sometimes show a ploughman and reaper, again emphasising the centrality of trade and commerce and the idea of fertility and fecundity of the region. As a whole, even under the Romans, the motifs on Alexandrian coinage maintained a very strong Egyptian iconographic theme.[41] Having constructed a picture of the organisation of the physical space of the city, and then overlaid the key and contradictory economic and social factors at work within it, let us now pay a little more attention to the identity of the actors themselves, and attempt to see how the idea of personal identity impacted upon the urban canvas.

URBAN SPACE AND ETHNIC IDENTITY: BEING AND BELONGING

We have already hinted earlier in this chapter when considering the political organisation of the city that democracy, although something emphasised by the Greeks, was not available to all. The idea of being an Alexandrian, or attaining legal status through formal citizenship, was a concept that was tightly bound to ethnicity; being 'Greek' was the most important thing in this regard. Attaining citizenship had a number of benefits. Even when the city came under Roman domination after the Augustinian elevation of Alexandria, all Alexandrian citizens were exempt from the general Roman poll tax;[42] citizenship then still emphasised the 'Greekness' of Alexandria, a sense of corporate identity defined upon the basis of all the traits that are bound up in that problematic label 'ethnicity': Greek language, Greek culture, but not necessarily Greek blood or genetic material. It is also clear that the native Egyptian was largely at the base of this social pyramid, but there were other ethnicities present in Alexandria too; the Jews were one of the most important social groups here, and although anti-semitism was not overt, Jews were excluded from the Gymnasium and on occasions inter-communal violence resulted in the destruction of Jewish property.

To be regarded as being a citizen of Alexandria, one's father and mother had to be Alexandrians and this decided access to a gymnasium or school. Beneath this elite layer we find a second social tier, Hellenes, who were other Greeks and Jews. In time, 'being Greek' would be a stepping stone to attaining Roman citizenship.[43] Even in Ptolemaic times, then, Alexandria was beginning to take on a very cosmopolitan outlook; Strabo speaks of not only a large Jewish population but also large groups of Persians and Syrians. Ptolemy Philadelphus even introduced Gaulish mercenaries into his army and this is supported by the names we find in funerary inscriptions of this period.[44] Ptolemaic Alexandria was in every sense a truly international city, but these identities were subsumed under one overarching label: this label 'Greekness' embodied a number of subtle nuances, it was not a matter of ethnicity alone. Let us consider now how we might infer ethnic identity from archaeological material, and take as a special case study the Jewish population of Alexandria.

From the very days of Moses himself, the Jewish people had formed attachments to the land of Egypt, and we find during Ptolemaic times a thriving Jewish mercantile community in Alexandria. This is not surprising given its proximity to the Levant and in any case a significant portion of the diaspora was scattered around the eastern Mediterranean basin. Apart from the obvious textual evidence, such as explicit mention of Jewish names, we do find outside of Alexandria itself a cultural testimony to the antiquity and scale of Jewish-Egyptian interaction. At Elephantine Island in Upper Egypt are the remains of a Jewish Temple and another important site is Tell el-Yahoudiya[45] in the Eastern Delta, approximately 20km (15 miles) north-east of Cairo. The Temple of Yahweh here was constructed by Onias III (an ousted high priest of Jerusalem) with the tacit approval of Ptolemy VI around 160 BC and was only finally closed under the orders of Vespasian in the late first century AD. It is clear then that Jewish people constituted an important element of the Egyptian population over hundreds of years.

Alexandria's Jewish population was not only numerically important, it was also responsible for one of the greatest feats of literature and religious scholarship: the production of a Greek version of the Old Testament (Septuagint). According to legend, 70 Rabbis were held on the Pharos island on the orders of Ptolemy II and all told to produce a Greek translation of the Hebrew scripture; miraculously all the 70 individual versions were exactly the same and thus was seen as a good omen (the Greek Old Testament–Septuagint–gets its name from these seventy Rabbis). There is no doubt that this was an important and trusted element of Ptolemaic Alexandrian society, but how do we account for their cultural affiliations and achievements in the context of cosmopolitan Alexandria? The identification of a Jewish presence in Hellenistic Alexandria has tested a number of scholars; some believe that the identity of the Jewish population was essentially shaped by Hellenistic contact, whilst other scholars see the idea of being Jewish and being a 'Hellene' fundamentally incompatible.[46] What is clear is that there are no neat boundaries; many of Egypt's Jews at this time readily accepted certain degrees of Hellenistic culture whilst not compromising their Jewish religious identity and belief, another example of the problems of defining ethnic identities through reference to material culture alone.

With this problem of ethnic syncretism in mind, how can we begin to strip bare the archaeology of the Jewish population of Hellenistic Alexandria? Our first step would be in the identification of the temple, as theoretically a Jewish place of worship should be a distinctive architectural form conforming wholly to the demands of ritual. It could not be confused, we would argue, applying a structuralist 'checklist' approach with another form of building. Is it really this easy? Synagogues are historically varied buildings reflecting a great deal of local tradition,[47] we know well from many contemporary sources that there was a massive colonnaded Alexandrian synagogue which was also the centre of considerable secular power, housing the gatherings of the local Jewish council, the *Politeuma*.[48] As an expression of considerable wealth and social power, this would have been a remarkable edifice, but we have no archaeological evidence for its appearance (this is a theme that is becoming familiar in relation to Alexandria's built heritage). Some indirect evidence of the synagogue's appearance may be found at a fifth-century AD mosaic at Beth Shean, Israel, which shows a colonnaded building as the synagogue may have looked before its destruction in AD 115-7,[49] but this is sadly as close as we can get. It will only be perhaps through a chance archaeological find in the future that we may finally discover concrete evidence for the place of worship of the city's Jews.

Are there any other avenues that will help us shed light upon the Jews of Alexandria? Mortuary evidence again affords some scope for identifying ideological practice, although we should approach such data with caution; the social and religious syncretism of contemporary Alexandria (*colour plate 1*) shows us just how hard it is to identify religious (or ethnic affiliation) through funerary evidence. We have the same problem when we attempt to deconstruct a notional Hellenistic burial practice. The physical evidence is not conclusive, although there are occasional clues; it is clear that alongside their Hellenistic neighbours, Jewish families favoured the standard loculus-type structure (a tomb with a central room with niches leading off). From the available evidence, and in common with contemporary Palestinian Jewish tomb structures, it does appear that unlike the Greek tombs, there does appear to be an absence of figural painting and relief in Alexandria's Jewish tombs.[50] It is also possible that the metropolitan Jews in Alexandria did practice cremation (as is noted in the Jewish tombs outside the city), but in general inhumation was the favoured form of disposal of the body.[51] Funerary inscriptions also furnish another avenue of enquiry: personal names. We find at the necropolis of El Ibrahimiyah, in tombs that may belong to Jewish soldiers, Greek forms of very obviously Hebrew names: for example Abramis for Abraham, Iosepos for Joseph and Iakoubis for Ya'akov.[52]

18 The modern synagogue in Alexandria now serves a much smaller congregation than in former times, yet bears witness to an enduring legacy of religious cosmopolitanism. *Sarah Finneran*

The funerary evidence clearly lends credence to the idea that the city's Jewish population freely accepted Hellenistic cultural norms in both life and in death; the funerary stelae generally copy the Hellenistic forms – even down to inscriptions making explicit reference to Graeco-Roman mythology – yet in no way did they forfeit this amorphous sense of Jewishness. The Jews of Alexandria played a full part in the cultural life of the city, including such Graeco-Roman pursuits as games and the theatre, yet they also developed their own thriving festival cycle in the ritual year; a festival on the Pharos commemorating the creation of the Septuagint was especially popular and the population was also able, according to their means, to engage in wide-ranging pilgrimage to ancestors' and heroes' tombs and temples in other lands (the context of pilgrimage is discussed more fully from a Christian perspective in chapter three). It is not clear how much the indigenous Egyptian culture was able to influence Egypt's Jewish population; in Alexandria the dynamic is clearly a Hellenistic–Judaic relationship with very little apparent input from the older native culture. This is explicable, in part, to the relative social positions of the ethnic groups involved; Jews were clearly at the core of the city's life in many areas and we have seen that native Egyptians were marginalised within the urban bureaucracy and social life, but one scholar has suggested that the boundaries between Egyptian and Jewish ritual practice were probably more permeable in Upper Egypt than in Alexandria or, say, Tell el-Yahoudiyah.[53]

On another scale, can we also speak of Jewish domestic space? Philo's *In Flaccum* is a key source of information surrounding the everyday life of Alexandria's Jewish community, but contrary to what we know of contemporary arrangements of domestic space in Judaea, where we may find archaeological examples of specific gendered spaces defined according to Judaic ritual principles, we cannot realistically recognise specifically Jewish domestic space. Jewish architecture beyond the synagogue conforms to Hellenistic and Roman 'rules',[54] but it also seems that we can identify certain artisan groups within the urban space who were devoted to carrying out functions associated *specifically* with Judaic Temple ritual; historical records show bakers producing bread specifically for festivals and Temple services, as well as incense makers – again something that would be used in the Jewish ritual cycle.[55] According to historical records, the Jewish population of Alexandria was concentrated near the eastern harbour ('Delta' quarter) and it is therefore probable that they were engaged heavily with trade and formed a significant part of the mercantile class; it does appear from some historical sources that in some cases they had cornered as a specialist trade the export and import of cloth and linen and tapestry manufacture.[56]

Although Jews were able to permeate the higher levels of Alexandrian society, the relationships between gentile and Jew were not always cordial. In Roman times, during the reign of the Emperor Trajan in AD 115-7, there was a bloody revolt of the city's Jews. In AD 116 Cyrenaican Jews from Libya attacked the city; this was an eschatological (i.e. apocalyptic) movement aiming at a return to Palestine and they hoped to enlist the support of the city's Jewish population,[57] but Zealots attacked the Serapeion and for a brief period there was a considerable popular backlash against the Jews. Graeco-Egyptian texts of the second and third centuries AD in particular paint the Jews in a less than sympathetic light, so it is clear that there was not always an idealised cosmopolitan harmony within Alexandria. Having considered the possibilities for the archaeological recognition of religious groups as ethic identities, let us now turn to a consideration of the primary ideological elements within the city: the Temple and Hellenistic religion.

HELLENISTIC SACRED SPACE

The early Ptolemies were enthusiastic temple builders; their world view was essentially an ancient Egyptian belief recast in a Greek form, and their newly created ritual spaces reflected to a degree this sort of syncretic outlook. Where the Ptolemies encouraged their images to be placed upon temple walls – like the pharaohs – the Romans followed; the temple became the meeting point of the different cosmological outlooks, but this happy equilibrium did not last.[58] The temple priesthood became steadily more Hellenised, thus alienating the native Egyptian priests who had been entrusted by the Ptolemies to serve the divine king in the Egyptian manner. This shift to a more overt Hellenistic outlook caused much nationalist resentment and culminated in a degree of religious unrest during the second century BC. These early Ptolemaic major temple constructions – which reached their apogee in the constructions down the Nile at Dendera and Philae – ushered in the idea of the cult of the ruler, a quasi-mythic status for the earthly king, a concept redolent of earlier pharaonic practice[59] and one which was helped actively and legitimised by the old Egyptian priesthood (and the suffix 'Soter', meaning saviour, clearly harked back to the protective aspects of the Horus king.[60])

Hellenistic architecture as a whole was ordered and rigid; it was, in the words of one authority, 'not the medium through which the artistic originality of the Hellenistic age was most effectively expressed'.[61] The Ptolemaic temple was designed to be the house of the god and to manifest his earthly power. Physically and emotionally these buildings were at the centre of urban life; they were designed clearly with ideas of monumentality in mind: they had to make a visual impact. As the city itself was based upon a grid, the temple complex itself conformed to certain metrical rules of geometry, but this was not to ignore or be closed to influence from outside, for even Plato himself had recognised the inherent beauty of Egyptian artistic forms.[62] The temple, more than anywhere, mediated the everyday secular life and the ideological sphere, it 'enclosed the visible image of a particular personage in the divine world'.[63] The Hellenistic temple complex was designed to make the body move through its sacred space in a very set way – in a sense one could suggest a ritual choreography. The layout of the architecture masked spaces and opened up other views, the natural world was almost framed within the strictures of sacred architecture; experiencing bodily the temple space was akin to experiencing the sensation of the labyrinth,[64] where heightened awareness was achieved through physical movement and bodily confusion. These buildings were dedicated to a very special set of gods, a syncretic meeting of the Greek and Egyptian worlds.

The Graeco-Egyptian pantheon was based on an amalgam of classical Greek and ancient Egyptian deities. Foremost among these within the Ptolemaic period was the cult of Serapis which developed under Ptolemy I[65] and was originally associated with the Serapeion at Memphis. Serapis was, in fact, an amalgamated deity that combined the worship of Osiris and Apis – the cult was formalised by a priest of Heliopolis named Manetho (his sacred texts would later be an important addition to the

19 Marble statuette of Serapis: an Egyptian divine personality rendered as a Greek god. *Alexandria, Graeco-Roman Museum. Sarah Finneran*

library at Alexandria)⁶⁶ – and the oldest Serapeion was at Saqqara (the Temple of Osorapis; the elision of both sacred names was later corrupted to form Serapis).

Within Alexandria the most important Ptolemaic sacred space was the Serapeion, a vast temple complex in what is now the Karmous district (around the site of Pompey's Pillar, see 6). The structure was built by Ptolemy III Euergetes in the late third century BC, and it followed the standard configuration of a Greek temple. Little remains of this building which clearly dominated the sacred space of the Ptolemaic city and must have formed the focus of the dedicated temple district, but to the west of Pompey's pillar one is able to view two limestone-lined subterranean galleries which may have been associated with the original installation; they may have acted as repositories for sacred scrolls or the mummies of sacred animals. Excavations on the site in the 1940s uncovered two phases of a colonnaded court building (some walls had been recorded by Mahmoud Bey in 1866). The temple itself was not approached along a longitudinal axis; the idea of the labyrinth alluded to earlier meant that the access in a Greek temple such as this was via an angle (not frontally, along a linear axis as would be the case in an Egyptian temple). This approach served to mask the actual sacred building from view, allowing for a swift 'revelation' rather than a measured approach – Egyptian temples made no secret of their physical dominance of space, the goal of the movement through the massive pylon gates and the colonnaded courtyard was the shrine of the deity.

It would, however, be a mistake to view this building as a direct Greek transplant; as with most elements of Alexandria's material culture all is not as it first appears. A number of foundation plaques of gold, silver, faience, glass and bronze, each bearing dedicatory Greek and Demotic inscriptions and dating to the reign of Ptolemy III are displayed in the Graeco-Roman Museum; this a feature of the Egyptian temple and is unknown in Greek constructions. The site of the Serapeion gives little clue to its former importance, although as a sacred space it was reused. The site of Pompey's pillar, which stands roughly on top of the main courtyard of the temple, actually represents an incoherent jumble of bits of Egypt's history translated wholly out of context; the sphinx at the base of the column probably dates from the reign of Ptolemy VI; there is a statue of the 25th-dynasty pharaoh Psammetichus I and at least two of the 19th-dynasty pharaoh Ramesses II, probably taken from Heliopolis,

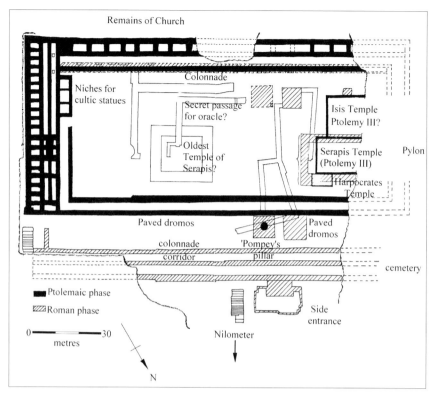

Remains of Church

Colonnade

Niches for
cultic statues

Secret passage
for oracle?

Isis Temple
Ptolemy III?

Oldest
Temple of
Serapis?

Serapis Temple
(Ptolemy III)

Pylon

Harpocrates
Temple

Paved dromos

Paved
dromos

colonnade
corridor

'Pompey's
pillar

cemetery

Ptolemaic phase

Roman phase

Side
entrance

0 ————— 30
metres

Nilometer

N

20 Excavations at the site of the Serapeion in the 1940s by Alan Rowe yielded evidence
of a number of phases of building on the site. Note on the south-western extremity
remains of an old church, testament to this idea of a syncretism of space. Partially redrawn
after A Rowe and B. Rees (1957) 'A contribution to the archaeology of the Western
Desert' *Bulletin of the John Rylands Library* 39: 485–520

and even the pillar itself has nothing to do with Pompey.[67] Undoubtedly
this was the centre of a hugely popular royal cult – apart from the original Serapeion at Saqqara and the large one at Alexandria, there was also
an installation down the coast at Abu Kir which subsequently became a
large pilgrim centre – but we have no concrete evidence of any other
Hellenistic temples in Alexandria (although there is a terracotta model of
a temple dedicated to the Egyptian deity Hathor in the Graeco-Roman
Museum which dates from around the second century BC). Archaeology
has largely failed us in the identification of cultic places, but a number of
Alexandrian coins dating from the Roman emperors Trajan and Hadrian
show not only varied representations of the Serapeion (an early issue

shows a façade with two Corinthian columns supporting a gabled roof), but also in some cases depict smaller Isis/Harpocrates shrines and portable shrines.[68]

The syncretic nature of Ptolemaic religion reflected the cosmopolitan nature of the city itself. A number of different cults were celebrated: Egyptian local deities, Olympian deities, dynastic cults, the Dionysus cult and also oriental cults such as Cybele (a Phrygian goddess of fertility), the Syrian cult of Atargatis and of course the Judaic religion. These different deities and their places of worship, whilst not archaeologically recognisable, are all attested by contemporary texts and inscriptions.[69] Again, we can only guess at the detailed aspects of these ceremonies and observances; although superficially it seems that we are dealing with a transplanted Greek cosmology grafted onto elements of ancient Egyptian religion, the picture is surely more complex. As Alexandria became a magnet for peoples from all over the wider region, so new beliefs were introduced and adapted; as new immigrants made their mark upon the secular space of the city, so the sacred space of the city changed too. Just as the London of today has different geographical areas associated with different distinctive immigrant ethnic groups, for example, so too did Alexandria. The definition of Alexandria's cosmopolitanism thus worked at many levels, but perhaps the one major theme that bound these disparate peoples together on a more common level was a Greek introduction: formalised learning.

CITY OF LEARNING

The ideal of education and science was closely associated with this new meeting of the Greek and Egyptian worlds and showed the possibility of extending the scope of learning by combining the best intellectual traditions of the two peoples. The cosmology of Ptolemaic Egypt (the way in which people sought to understand how their world functioned) was certainly bound up in the quest for secular knowledge. It is clear that education played a highly important part in Greek life and these ideals were latterly translated into the Graeco-Roman milieu. The goal of education was not solely didactic; in the words of one scholar 'education was an agent for preserving 'Greekness' by maintaining fixed linguistic and social boundaries excluding almost any form of Egyptian culture',[70] but this was not followed in practice. In cosmopolitan Alexandria at least, the best ideas of the Egyptians were admitted to the intellectual sphere as much as the Egyptian religious elements were combined with the Greek. The educational system actively sought to maintain the notion of Greek ethnic and cultural identity in Alexandria, but there was room here for a syncretism of ideas and a meeting of minds and in time Hellenistic Alexandria became the epitome of teaching and research in a wide variety of fields. What evidence do we have for the centrality of education in the lives of the Alexandrians?

Textual evidence for education in Graeco-Roman Egypt is particularly plentiful, indicating the supreme importance and emphasis placed on the idea of learning and teaching; how is this reflected in the archaeological record? The actual place for teaching was known as the *didaskaleia*, and this meant 'school' in the loosest sense of the word as there was no dedicated space for learning. 'Schools' met in temples or even in tombs – essentially an *ad hoc* arrangement of teaching space primarily emphasising the need to stay cool in the heat of the day. We can find traces of the material culture of learning in many buildings; on the walls of the Temple of Hathor at Dendera, for example, the names of important festive days are inscribed on the wall – here was the blackboard for the class.[71] In rare cases even the writing materials of the scholars have been preserved, such as reed pens, as well as pottery sherds – *ostraka* – used as exercise books.[72]

The more formalised Greek *Gymnasia* had their origins in Athens as early as the fourth century BC; soon they too were widespread in Ptolemaic Egypt, although latterly in Roman times they tended to be restricted to the actual *Nome* capitals. The system for education was set out from an early age; pedagogues – who essentially became an extension of the family unit, a sort of live-in *au pair* – taught the youngest children. There then followed a programme of primary education with an intensive secondary education to follow. It should be noted that certain teachers were in great demand and occupied niches indicative of a high social standing, although as a rule they represented the whole social spectrum and there were also a number of important female teachers.

When we think of Alexandria as a city of learning, we tend to forget the sort of urban scholastic establishment described above and think most of all of the famous Mouseion – the temple to the muses – an unrivalled centre of ancient learning located in all probability opposite the tomb of Alexander, at the spiritual centre of the city on the Street of the Soma.[73] This library (research institution, in the modern sense, might be a better concept) was created on the orders of Ptolemy I; he appointed as librarian Demetrius of Phaleron and instructed him to gather as many manuscripts as he could, using every strategy imaginable, in order to form the largest ever corpus of research materials covering the whole range of human scholastic endeavour. The ideal of the library had been an important feature of Greek culture and the concept was now enthusiastically embraced by Ptolemy I, anxious to prove the elevated cultural status of Alexandria. Demetrius scoured the Mediterranean for books on all scientific and artistic topics, from Greece and from native Egyptian historiographic sources – especially the legendary sacred records of the High Priest Manetho.

It is important to emphasise here that the library did not deal solely with Greek or Egyptian material, it emphasised a unity of knowledge, and as such promoted a very syncretic *intellectual* outlook.[74] Often manuscripts were stolen to order and many were removed from ships berthed in the harbour; this voracious acquisitions strategy was exceptionally successful, so much so that Ptolemy III was forced to build a smaller 'daughter' library at the Serapeion to house a portion of the estimated 400,000 scrolls acquired by means of plunder and purchase.[75] The Mouseion soon rivalled the reputations of Aristotle's Lyceum and Plato's Academy back in Greece, and gathered here, in this premier research institution (it should be noted that initially at least there was little formal teaching, *per se*) were some of the finest minds the Greek world had produced: Eratosthenes, a mathematician who deduced, on the basis of the differential length of the shadows cast by obelisks at midday in different parts of Egypt, that the earth was not flat, and on the basis of this observations made a very accurate estimate of its circumference, and other resounding names in many branches of the sciences and humanities such as Euclid, Archimedes and the Geographer Claudius Ptolemy.

The architecture of the Mouseion emphasised its multi-disciplinary role; built along the lines of an Egyptian Ramesses temple, it was a combination of palace, museum and shrine. The grandeur of the architecture reflected the premium upon which the rulers placed learning, it was a beacon of Greek culture, and whilst Egyptian ideas could be admitted, it was in every sense an advertisement for the Hellenistic achievement. There were vast storage areas for the library scrolls and small attached rooms for teaching. The shrine served an important function; although dedicated to the muses, and symbolically linking the sacred and secular worlds, the idea of the addition of a religious element was borrowed from Plato's original Athenian school, where a school required a degree of religious status in order to gain protection under Athenian law. The community (*synodos*) centred upon the library comprised 30-50 male scholars who were entitled to free lodgings and exempt from paying tax. Alexandria, then, saw the meeting of Greek and Egyptian concepts of space, religion and scholarship, a true intellectual syncretism. To some extent this cosmopolitanism is also reflected in ideas about Alexandrian art, where again we see a meeting of the Egyptian and Greek aesthetic.

THE ALEXANDRIAN AESTHETIC

Artistically, the history of Greek interaction with Egypt had seen a borrowing of Egyptian concepts of representation and architectural space. The earliest trading settlements in the Delta, such as Naucratis and Daphnae, used a number of Egyptian architectural features in the design of their public buildings.[76] Further afield, we find on the Island of Delos in the Aegean the famous seventh-century BC marble Lion statues; dedicated to Apollo, in the eyes of many scholars they embody clear Egyptian representational influences (*21*)[77] and similar traits may also be traced in sixth-century BC Spartan art. Hellenistic artistic convention is truly syncretic; here we find the origins of the overflown baroque, and themes of burlesque, humour and the grotesque;[78] but apart from this seeming acceptance and embracing of cosmopolitan ideas, Hellenistic depictions also emphasised an introspective approach, in the words on one authority this is 'the first period in the history of western art in which a serious attempt was made to probe, capture and express through the mechanisms of portraiture the inner workings of the human mind'.[79]

The very cosmopolitan nature of Alexandria produced a 'tolerance for difference' that provided yet another dimension to the Hellenistic artistic form.[80] One specialisation of the Alexandrian workshops during Ptolemaic times was the 'grotesque'; these were small, bronze figures of crippled beggars or hunchbacks and their popularity suggests a reaction against the wholesome and uncritical idea of beauty. It is also important to point out that the artistic conventions of the time embraced the pos-

21 One of the fabled Lions from the Aegean Island of Delos. Dating from the seventh century BC, their appearance is reminiscent of Egyptian statuary, especially in the crouched stance. Here we may have evidence for the beginnings of a combined Greek/Egyptian aesthetic even before the advent of Alexander the Great. *Niall Finneran*

sibility of depicting the 'other' in terms of different ethnic groups, again reflecting the overall cosmopolitan composition of Alexandria's population.[81] In a sense one could argue that Alexandria, on the interface of Africa and Europe, took Hellenistic art and recast it to reflect the day to day realities of life There. It is tempting to almost suggest that the circumstances of its manufacture, recoiling against rigid convention, and mass-producing in some cases what we could today recognise as 'kitsch', were the epitome of the post-modern aesthetic.

But we should not lose sight of the fact that this wry way of looking at the world was just one method of depiction. At the other end of the aesthetic scale we also see an emphasis on the idea of the heroic and charismatic; kings and leaders striking poses, warriors seated upon horses;[82] similar 'heroic' subjects included famous athletes, orators and philosophers. Gods too were rendered in heroic poses. Serapis, for instance, was definitely modelled upon a prototype cultic statue by an artist called Bryaxis and was depicted as a throned, draped figure with a frontal aspect and a full beard, just like Zeus, in fact (see *19*).[83] In terms of cultic statuary there was a marked lack of artistic syncretism in Alexandria, unlike in the *Chora* where there is more scope for individual choice on the part of the artist and increasing emphasis on native Egyptian iconographic schemes.[84] In the rural lands, for some reason, perhaps being nearer to the primeval Egyptian ideological outlook, the artisans were willing to admit more of an aesthetic amalgam of representation. The countryside represented more artistic freedom, without the constraints of the urban consumer.

The Hellenistic sculpture of Alexandria tells us much about how the ruling classes saw themselves. Favoured scenes include tableaux, feasts and grand processions. The Touk el-Karamous treasure dating from the third century BC and discovered in the Nile Delta in 1905 shows the full cosmopolitan range of the Hellenistic cultural taste; here we find Persian-style Rhyton drinking cups with gryphon depictions,[85] Egyptian themes and Greek subjects. We have now considered broadly the variety of the Alexandrian cultural experience, and it is clear that a similar theme constantly recurs: the amalgamation of ideas and motifs, of peoples, of ideas, true cosmopolitanism. At the interface of the Greek and Egyptian worlds the foregoing discussion illustrates how we cannot impose rigid analytical boundaries; structural and functional analysis of a place such as this cannot work. I would argue that we are dealing with what would today be termed a 'post-modernist' phenomenon (before modernism even existed!). The classical Greek paradigm was recast with an Egyptian flavour, shifting of meanings, syncretism of place and space. We have isolated the single physical phenomenon of the Greek interface and impact with the Egyptian world and seen how notions of culture and identity were essentially deconstructed. Let us now add another cultural variable to the equation.

ROMANISATION OF HELLENIC SPACE

Octavian's defeat of Antony and Cleopatra brought Egypt formally into the Roman world; politically and socially it was now integrated into the most important socio-political and economic bloc in the world, but did Rome change Alexandria or did Alexandria change Rome? Again we find a dual dynamic, a two-way relationship, and yet again shifts in social and political and ideological allegiances are clear in the construction of urban space. In the first place, the Romans were clear that somehow Alexandria did not belong to the rest of Egypt. Within the broader administrative framework of the state much of the Ptolemaic organisation of space remained intact. Essentially the native Egyptian still remained at the base of the social pyramid, in the words of one authority as much as the native Indian was under the British *Raj*.[86] The Emperor's direct representative was the *Praefectus Alexandriae et Aegypti* (again this title show the anomalous role, administratively speaking, of the city itself), and the next layer of bureaucracy brought together representatives of the civil law and religion. The Greek cities of Naucratis, Alexandria, Ptolemais and Antinoë were governed separately from the rest of Egypt, the *Chora*. In Alexandria, supreme legal control was vested in the *archidicastes*, the chief justice or master of the rolls who looked after the administration of the *Katologeion*, the record office of legal judgements.

The Romans tended to retain a number of important bureaucratic elements of the Alexandrian administrative apparatus, and this general air of acceptance of the *status quo* was maintained across the urban structure, although some modifications were made. Augustus feared all along that Egypt could potentially be used as an effective base for political opposition, and as such the reins of power there were tightened, resulting in less latitude than elsewhere in the Empire; the governor, for instance, was an equestrian praefectus rather than a senator, and Augustus also banned senators from travelling freely around Egypt.[87] The Romans also modified the Ptolemaic 'suburbs' and reorganised urban social space; membership of these areas continued to be based upon the idea of hereditary registration in the group (*Deme*).

Alexandria retained a great economic importance too. In terms of financial administration, at the earliest opportunity the Romans reorganised the Alexandrian coinage and the value of the silver tetradrachm was pegged to that of the universal denarius. For the rest of Egypt a poll tax was introduced but this did not affect the citizens of Alexandria (or on the wider scale, slaves).[88] Alexandria was regarded as somehow being not part of Egypt; this idea of otherness, fostered in the first place by the founding Greeks, was continued, and the city was seen as being, in the words of Bowman and Rathbone, a sort of quasi 'allied state' with important economic and strategic interests for Rome. Alexandria was organised along different lines in terms of government, taxation and cultural life, and whereas an Egyptian could not aspire to Roman citizenship, an Alexandria citizen could, and would expect to play a part in the wider Roman cultural world (this was later revoked in AD 212 under the *Constitutio Antoniniana*). Subsequently the Alexandrian model for urban governance would be transferred to other cities in Egypt; the division into clan-based districts and the presence of an elite gymnasium-based group. As a consequence, when the real municipalisation of Egypt began under Augustus, Alexandrian administrators were much in demand in the *Chora*.

This Roman reorganisation had some profound effects; in time Alexandria began to lose its identity as an Egyptian city. Whereas in Ptolemaic times we do see a happy acceptance of the best that pharaonic Egypt had to offer; initially, under the Romans, Alexandria enjoyed a privileged position, but it had to be fully integrated into the Roman world at all costs. There could be no acceptance of native influences. In 215, the Emperor Caracalla, believing that Egyptians had been implicated in the murder of his brother Geta, expelled all Egyptians from the city.[89] This was a complete and ruthless act that today could be described as ethnic cleansing. With this act the nature of the city changed: culturally, socially and ideologically.

Another important action was the incorporation of the temples within the Roman administrative structure; the religious framework of Egypt was controlled perhaps more closely than in any other part of the Empire,[90] and the political power of the priesthood was therefore considerably reduced, yet day-to-day economic and ideological life was still focused upon the temple building.[91] The Serapeion was remodelled by the Romans with the enlargement of the colonnade in around 181 and then again in 217; portions of the original Ptolemaic structure were restored and the complex was generally extended (of particular architectural note is the use of concrete in the foundations). It is also possible that the Romans restored the pre-Ptolemy III Serapis temple at the library end of the complex for Isis worship.[92] Again archaeology alone cannot tell us much of the physical appearance of these temples (as is the case with earlier Ptolemaic cultic foundations), but occasionally we can recognise buildings on the designs of Roman coins; this is especially true of the Isis temple.[93] As for the Serapeion, it has been described in the words of one author as being comparable stylistically to 'Herod's Temple at Jerusalem', possessing a high elevation on a platform surrounded by colonnades.⁹⁴ Judith McKenzie has made an excellent attempt at reconstructing the appearance of the Serapeion during Roman times; as noted above, the Roman version was a larger temple space, with an extended colonnaded courtyard; a stairway in the east side of the courtyard covered the Ptolemaic Nilometer, and foundation deposits of coins were found in the pool near the eastern entrance. A *lageion* or racecourse lay to the south of the newly modelled Serapeion.⁹⁵

The Romans reused and enhanced Ptolemaic sacred space and also made their own contribution to urban monumentality. Pompey's Pillar (it was given the name by the Crusaders) within the sacred precinct itself was probably dedicated by the Prefect to the Emperor Diocletian in around 297, and was probably topped by a porphyry statue; this is not to be seen today, although the top of the pillar (which is a 27m-high shaft of red granite) is quite spacious, and according to legend 22 people were able to dine on the top in 1832! Constantine closed the Serapeion in 325, and historical sources suggest that it remained relatively intact until 391 when it was finally destroyed by the Christians and a church dedicated to John the Baptist was subsequently erected on the site. We will consider the nature of syncretism of space more closely in the next chapter, but at this stage it is worth reflecting that certain locales within the urban zone retained a great degree of inherent symbolism. The Romans tended not to build cultic installations anew; the same spaces retained importance across the centuries.

The worship of Augustus (again note the link with the idea of a divine king, a much earlier Egyptian idea) was centred upon the Caesareum complex, which was located roughly in the area of the modern Zaghloul Square at the northern end of the Street of the Soma. Two obelisks – brought from Aswan – flanked the entrance; their presence indicates the explicit link that the Romans wished to make with Egypt's pharaonic past; as Cleopatra's Needles they now stand on the Embankment in London and in Central Park New York, making, indeed, another colonialist statement. This complex was completed by the architect Pontius (although it had been instituted initially by Cleopatra and Julius Caesar), and was without doubt one of the most important religious and indeed political centres in all of Roman Egypt. Nothing of the Caesareum survives, and it is difficult to reconstruct the Roman sacred city on the basis of current archaeological evidence. Where we do have the remains of a Roman temple, we owe a debt of good luck and fortune; in 1936, during building work, the Temple at Ras es-Soda – a private dedication to Isis and probably dating from around the second century AD – was found by complete chance. It is probable that other temples will come to light only in such fortuitous circumstances.

What do we know about monumentality and building in Roman Alexandria? In terms of overall architectural style, a distinctive Romanised Alexandrian flavour soon emerged in the first two centuries of the first millennium AD; many essentially Hellenistic 'baroque' elements, such as ornate capital details – a key Alexandrian motif – survived and indeed flourished in Roman times. We certainly know that Alexandrian master builders were in great demand across the Roman Empire; *Mechanikoi* or architects' texts spanning the period of the first century BC to the sixth century AD indicate the great social status of these artisans, and the sort of cachet they commanded.[96] As has been continually emphasised, we only have fragmentary remains of buildings from Roman Alexandria (which we will discuss below), and for a better picture of Roman town architecture and urban planning we should really look to the other important towns of Antinoë or Hermopolis Magna.[97] Perhaps the most detailed picture of the evolution of domestic space and architecture in Egypt in Roman times is furnished by the excavations at Karanis; here we see the standard form of urban domestic architecture and spatial configuration where the street patterns would seem to indicate a structure loosely based on the idea of the neighbourhood. There are also considerable typological variations in house types at Karanis; there is not a uniform domestic type of architectural space. The structuration of domestic space may be a result of the property being divided among surviving children as an inheritance, because in some cases we see a continual fragmentation of living space. In this sense, the ordering of architectural space mirrored social life,[98] the lifecycle reflected in architectural order.

How does this picture as yielded by excavation at Karanis square with what is known at Alexandria? Fortunately we do have at hand some exceptionally valuable archaeological evidence to help us. The Polish Kom el-Dikka excavations have provided us with perhaps the most detailed picture of domestic space in Roman Alexandria, essentially overlapping with the Byzantine period (we will discuss the implications of some of the material from these excavations in the next chapter).[99] In this suburb, it is clear that from the fifth century onwards that the architecture is redolent of comfortable wealth; 'villa-style' houses are

22 The theatre in the Kom el-Dikka area. *Sarah Finneran*

well appointed, and their spatial focus is a well-constructed and spacious peristyle court (such architectural forms may also be seen at locations such as Kellis and Abu Mina). Walls of some of these buildings are made in the distinctive *opus alexandrinum* style of rectangular panels painted red and yellow, and framed with black and green bands. Every amenity is here; the theatre, for instance was built in the second century as an Odeon to accommodate about 700 people and it is Egypt's only surviving example of a Graeco-Roman theatre, and there is also an extensive bath complex dating from the second century.

The arrangement of the houses in the area of street R4, however, seems not to emphasise the individual, but stresses spatially a communal living need; In House D, for instance, which was occupied between the third and fourth centuries AD, the small cellular rooms are of equal size, suggesting a commune of some sort, with emphasis on maximising private space. It has been suggested this house might represent an urban monastery – given the associated frescoes (discussed in chapter three below) not a surprising assumption – but other authorities suggest that these were communal artisans' quarters. These blocks of dwellings are grouped, in the Roman model of urban space, into the *Amphoda* (an idea that may be roughly translated as neighbourhood). Special interest attaches to the so-called 'Villa of the Birds', which is located (unusually given its obvious opulence) to the south of the theatre. This is clearly an elite structure, as witnessed by the range of magnificent mosaics. In cities of the *Chora* such neighbourhoods are recognisable archaeologically, they are obviously delineated, but in Alexandria the paucity of the available evidence does not allow us to recognise clear and distinct neighbourhoods or quarters.[100] The ceramic corpus yielded from these excavations is evidence for a wide range of trading contacts across the eastern Mediterranean, and the cosmopolitan nature of Alexandria society as a whole.[101]

The Romans sought to bring their organisational and engineering capabilities to improve domestic life in Alexandria. Water would have been a key commodity; as in common with many Roman cities, an extensive and developed water-distribution system was built in Alexandria. Many of these cisterns were in use as late as the nineteenth century, and they are found all over the city – even under the Nabi Daniel mosque where there is a particularly fine plastered example. The Shallalat cisterns are exceptionally spacious; built on three levels, these cisterns would have been filled annually during the Nile flood (the hydrology of the city at this time was still tied to that of the main river), but the inundation resulted in the wash through of large quantities of silt and keeping these cisterns clear of debris and detritus was an important task. Water was brought into the city via a canal tapping into the Canopic branch of the Nile at Shedya, roughly following the line of the later Mahmudiyah Canal. Having left their mark on the city of the living, the Romans also tapped into the Hellenistic heritage for their treatment of the afterlife.

We have already considered how change in the ideological fabric of the city may be reflected in traditions of burial. By and large, the Alexandrian urbanite of the Hellenistic and Roman city would be buried in dedicated subterranean cemetery areas:[102] *necropoleis* (literally cities of the dead). The standard burial complex comprised a *hypogeum* with several *loculi* (side chambers) running off the main room where individual niches for corpses were placed. We have seen that the most important cemetery site, placed in the Street of the Soma, was the royal mausoleum, traditionally the burial place of Alexander himself, and it

23 *Right:* The multi-storied water cisterns at El Nabih. Structures like these guaranteed the city a regular and plentiful water supply. *Geoffrey Tassie*

24 *Below:* Inside the Kom es-Shoqafa catacomb. *Sarah Finneran*

was here that the royal corpses were placed (this site retained a great deal of significance into Roman times too).

The Kom es-Shoqafa Necropoleis tomb complex is one of the best known of the city's and was in use from the first to the fourth centuries AD. The structure is accessed via a large rotunda, and beneath are several loculi arranged over a number of levels. South of the rotunda is a large room for funerary feasts (*triclinium*) which has benches cut into the walls around what would presumably have been a wooden table. East of the rotunda is a large tomb known as the Hall of Caracalla which strangely contained a large number of horse bones. In the architecture of these discrete family tombs we can really see syncretism at work; the sarcophagi, whilst Greek in design, tend to be decorated with Egyptian scenes and the mouldings and reliefs around the tombs show a mix of Greek and Egyptian iconography. The nearby Tigrane and Wardian tombs have similar iconographic schemes showing this complex mix of imagery and date from the first century AD.

The necropolis at Anfushi, on the western point of the Pharos Island at Ras el-Tin dates from around the second century BC, and is notable for some exceptionally fine frescoes; the juxtaposition of the Greek and Egyptian motifs within the funerary art is particularly interesting in Tomb I, where there is a real fusion of motifs. Humans are represented with faces in obviously Hellenistic style, (emphasising the naturalistic), yet their costume is obviously ancient Egyptian. Greek, Bacchic scenes adorn the funeral chambers juxtaposed with more sober, formalised Egyptian funerary scenes.[103] The Gabbari necropolis was uncovered during rescue excavation in 1997; again the design conforms to the Hellenistic model,[104] and here we find some evidence for cremation (which was taboo for Egyptians and latterly Christians).

At Chatby, in the east-central part of the city, the third-century BC necropolis area has been left open (*colour plate 10*). The main tomb is perhaps planned along the lines of a Greek house;[105] the obvious metaphor – and it is a common one – is that the tomb is a physical house for the deceased. The structure comprises an entrance, a hallway, a court and *prostas* (front room) leading into a burial chamber (*oikos*). In some cases, cremation was practised. This is witnessed by a type of jar known as the Hadra urn, which dates from around the third century BC, and is usually decorated with geometric motifs in purple, black or red; inscriptions often give the name and occupation of the deceased and it also

25 Inside the Anfushi catacombs, Ras el-Tin; tombs with exceptionally fine frescoes. *Sarah Finneran*

appears in some cases that the bone fragments remaining after cremation were deposited in a structured way within the urn.[106] The Hellenistic sarcophagus form proved to be remarkably resilient; this took the form of a coloured plaster imitation of a mattress with shaped wooden legs.[107] Also on the eastern edge of the city is the Necropolis of Mustafa Kamil, which dates from the third century AD.

So, the Romans, like the Greeks before them, adapted elements of Egyptian cosmology to form an essentially syncretic ideological outlook. But this was not the case with the city of the living; secular space was managed, reformed and redeveloped. The differences between the outlooks of the Ptolemies and Romans towards the city they ruled over are marked. In the Ptolemaic system there was no concept of private property, the economy was rigidly state controlled, there was exceptional technological development and a salaried, centralised state bureaucracy.

26 Funerary art from Kom es-Shoqafa (1). These scenes are obviously influenced by the funerary iconography of the Pharaohs (showing Anubis, the jackal-headed god of embalming) almost two thousand years earlier… yet the tomb commemorates a Greek. *Sarah Finneran*

27 Funerary art from Kom es-Shoqafa (2). Here we see clear Greek influences in the figurative statuary, especially in the delicate facial depiction and the hairstyle. *Sarah Finneran*

In Roman times, whilst we begin to see elements of private ownership emerging, technological developments were essentially stagnant and the bureaucracy was being decentralised. It was against this socio-economic background that we see the emergence of Christian society in Alexandria, a development that would have a profound effect upon the Roman Empire as a whole and the ordering and conception of urban space in the city.[108]

three

CHRISTIANITY AND COSMOPOLITANISM IN LATE ANTIQUE ALEXANDRIA

Religious syncretism and the cosmopolitan inheritance of the Hellenistic world blurred ritual boundaries within the urban space of Alexandria; we have already seen the variety of cults and religions that were celebrated under the aegis of the Ptolemies and then the Romans, but the mid-first century AD marked the beginnings of wider uncertainties, and from the near east a new way of worship and *way of life* was emerging. The impact of Christianity upon the Roman world cannot be underestimated: socially, economically, culturally and ideologically the advent of this powerful and dynamic new religion changed the face of the Mediterranean world. Just as the Hellenistic and Roman ritual world was reflected in the organisation of the city, so too did this new cosmological outlook impact upon the urban space of Alexandria, ushering in an era of intercommunal violence, factional infighting and a move to colonise the rural spaces beyond the boundaries of the city, overcoming that traditional dichotomy of nature and culture and desert and town through the action of the Christianisation of space.

What do we mean by this term 'Christianisation'? We have already touched upon the idea of the Hellenisation of Egyptian space, a physical planting of a Greek-style urban space in an Egyptian setting with its attendant socio-cultural shifts, and we may also possibly speak of a Romanisation of space, an attempt to reorder Alexandria politically and economically in the image of the Roman way of life. But the process of Christianisation is more subtle, and from an archaeological perspective less obvious. We will consider this point later in this section when we consider how archaeology alone can help us unravel the culture-history of Christianity in Alexandria and its hinterland, but first a caveat. The term 'Christianisation' has its opponents; it may be regarded as being too absolute, a process that has a definable end when there really should not be one. Philosophically the idea would be regarded as being teleological (a criticism levelled at Marxism, where the Marxist society is held up to be the finalised and idealised end point of social evolution). This is a valid criticism but, as we have already seen from the story so far, there are no neat boundaries, the city is always in a state of flux. There is no end point to the Christianisation of Alexandria's space; in places it is still ongoing, side by side with an Islamicisation of space and indeed a gathering secularisation of space. I take this idea to mean, in its simplest form, that we can recognise, from the material culture alone, the transition in dominant ideology from a patchwork of syncretic 'pagan' religions to a predominantly monolithic and inclusive religion (be it Christianity or Islam). At no point can we speak of a Christian revolution: the accent is upon a gradual social evolution.

At this juncture it would also be important to be clear about our use of these often problematic names. Christian Alexandria was a product of Hellenistic and Roman Alexandria, we may also refer to late antique Alexandria, or Byzantine Alexandria, or early medieval Alexandria. Such labels would also apply on the wider scale to the periodisation of the rather understudied post-pharaonic Egypt. We must be aware of applying labels that betoken religious affiliation to chronologically periodise our narrative. Alexandria is still Christian, it is also Islamic, and it is (rarely) still Jewish. The religious developments discussed in this chapter may best be understood as belonging to that amorphous 'late antique' period, at a point when the certainties of the classical world were eroding, and there was very much a sense of finality about the Roman world in the west. This is true of the east; the first half of the first millennium AD saw huge political and social flux in the eastern Mediterranean. The fragmentation of the Roman Imperial monolith, a focus of new political power centred upon Constantinople rather than Rome, inexorable Persian pressure from the east and the rise of Islam in the deserts of Arabia. In the west 'barbarian' Germanic tribes pressured the Rhine frontier. The story of the rise and ultimate triumph of Christianity in the Roman world belongs to this period of social and political change.

DAY BY DAY CALENDAR COMPANY

SALE   4746   115   0748   10-29
              REL 7.9/1.08   90   12:08

01 0767139887   12.9
                SUBTOTAL   12.9
VIRGINIA 5.0% TAX   .6
                TOTAL   13.6
XXXXXXXXXXXX1316 VISA   13.6
              PV# 0150748
XXXXXXXXXXXXXX OFFLINE XXXXXXXXXXXX

EXCHANGES ONLY - NO CASH REFUNDS

CUSTOMER RECEIPT

Crucially there is another label that demands our attention here; all too often the word 'pagan' is rather uncritically used to denote non-Christian traditional adherents of the long-established polytheistic (and in rare occasions monotheistic) religions of the Roman Empire, its contemporaries and antecedents. Looking over the biography of Alexandria, for instance, we find the term used extensively (and indeed it has been within this book too) when we speak of 'pagan' survivals, 'pagan' philosophers, 'pagan' temples or 'pagan' thought. Traditionally it has been accepted that the word pagan derives from the Latin *paganus* meaning rural-dweller or country person. The implication here, as suggested by the historian Ronald Hutton,[1] is clear and it draws upon the structural dichotomy between city and country, culture and nature. The city is perceived to be Christian, cultured ('urbane') whilst the countryside is heathen, backward and superstitious, but Hutton points out (according to a recent study by the French historian Pierre Chuvin) that the word merely denotes adherents the religion of the *pagus* (the local government unit) who preferred to follow the 'old' religious system. It is not a value judgement.

Let us now try to understand the history of Christianity in relation to Alexandria. The New Testament mentions only rarely the presence of Egyptians amongst the early Christian communities of the Roman east; we hear specifically of Jews from Alexandria in *Acts of the Apostles* 6:9, and in *Acts* 18: 24. Apollos, a colleague of St Paul at Ephesus and Corinth is mentioned as being a 'Jew of Alexandria' (an important social observation given the power and prestige enjoyed by Alexandria's Jewish community), but by and large Acts tends to ignore Alexandria – a surprising omission given the city's obvious socio-economic and political power at this time. The contrast with, say, Antioch, is surprising. Occasionally Roman records can offer some clarification of the situation in the mid-first century AD; a letter from Emperor Claudius to the Alexandrians in AD 41, for instance, warns against unnamed Jews 'from Syria' entering the city and engaging in preaching evidently new and subversive ideas.[2] Are these people Christians, or are they adherents of some unknown other radical Jewish sect?

Egyptian tradition states that Christianity was introduced into Egypt by the Apostle St Mark (*15, colour plate 11*), who converted an Alexandrian shoemaker by the name of Annianus; this presents something of a problem. Eusebius' Church History, a very important source for understanding the early Christian world, suggests that Mark arrived in Alexandria in AD 43, yet Annianus was only converted in 62. How can we account for this delay of 20 years? What was Mark doing in the meantime? Did he succeed in converting other citizens of Alexandria during this time? We do know that Annianus subsequently became the bishop of Alexandria upon the death of Mark, so he was evidently a person of some high standing, thus meriting a mention in the early texts. St Mark subsequently met a fate common to the early evangelists working in a predominantly hostile environment. He was martyred on the occasion of a festival day in honour of Serapis at a place called Boucalis (meaning oxen pasture) on the east of the town, probably near to the modern library. The place subsequently became a shrine (martyrium) and one of the most important pilgrimage centres in Christendom.

Before considering the many levels at which the urban and surrounding space of Alexandria was 'Christianised', we need to consider the dynamics of the conversion process as revealed through textual and material culture studies. We have already considered how the Greeks and Romans manufactured and recast the city space to reflect their own varied cosmological outlooks. This was done from on high, so to speak, and largely through the use of coercion: powerful military force backed up political will. Ideological meanings of space and place could be changed quickly on the say so of the political powers in charge: festival days, statues, places of worship, all were subject to the control of the political elite, and ideology could be used as a powerful mobilising force for a restless population. This was more than a case of divine power; secular power was vested in the control of the ideological system, the means by which the largely uneducated urban masses made sense of their world and their place in it (anthropologists term this cosmology).

The Christianisation of space was, in comparison, more subtle and a much longer-term process that reflected the relative social standing of the Christian population in Alexandria. The act of Christianisation, prior to Constantine's Edict of Toleration in 313, did not occur as part of a political process; in Alexandria – as in many areas of the Roman Empire – Christianity was a creed enthusiastically embraced initially among the lower cadres of society; their scope for influencing change was limited. Where Christianity was adopted by the ruling elites – and there are many examples from the late antique/early medieval periods such as: the Aksumite Empire of northern Ethiopia, the Caucasian kingdoms of

Armenia and Georgia, and in Anglo-Saxon England the Kingdom of Kent (we may also refer to any number of African kingdoms encountered by nineteenth-century European missionaries) – the impact of Christianity both culturally and socially would be almost immediate and all embracing. The first Christians of Alexandria, living against a background of continual persecution, kept a low profile for the first three centuries AD, only attaining a degree of legal and political power after 313.

The fact that the first Alexandrian Christians had to remain relatively invisible means that in terms of material culture, the archaeology of early Christianity in Alexandria (as in many areas of the Roman Empire) is a fragmentary and sparse, but when Christianity did attain a level of legal protection and political support, change was swift and in some cases the pace of change was so profound that intercommunal violence ensued. Christianity rapidly attracted new converts among all levels of Alexandrian society, but what was so appealing about this new message? Why was the rich 'pagan' classical cultural tradition of this city abandoned so readily? The process of conversion is complex and multi-layered, and there are no simple answers. In many cases the motivations for conversion may have been financial or purely coercive, an attempt to gain a political power base or influence.[3] In Alexandria much social and cultural power was vested in the classical philosophical tradition, and it is apparent that many attitudes proved hard to change. Now Alexandria's cosmopolitan outlook, the spirit of openness, an acceptance of the best that every cosmological viewpoint could offer, turned sour. Christianity was in essence a religion that was largely unable to admit syncretic ideas from elsewhere, there was only one prescribed way of living and worshipping: the example of Jesus' life was paramount and this perspective resulted in a departure from a climate of acceptance to one of more entrenched attitudes, often culminating in direct action and violence against followers of other religions. How can we trace this process, this shifting of identity, the acquisition of a new world view at odds with Alexandria's traditional spirit of free enquiry?

The process of Christianisation is evidenced socially and culturally on many levels. Textual studies have helped us gauge the uptake of the new religion in the form of the adoption of Christian names; it has been suggested that by the end of the fourth century the majority of the population whose names had been recorded on papyrological records were Christian, although these records may present an uneven view of the whole society.[4] Of more interest (from the point of view of the current study) is in the idea of the reordering of the urban environment to reflect the new ideological outlook. We can analyse this idea on two scales: place and space.

We have many examples from all over the late antique world of the seizure of pre-existing sacred places (temples) and their conversion into Christian churches. Christianity is not exactly a religion that is close to the idea of the natural place – arguably the closest we come is the use of the river as a baptismal pool, but in time, in the shape of the font and the baptistery building, this natural feature would be acculturated, brought physically into the church building and controlled. Pagans were much more attuned to the symbolism of natural features; from a phenomenological perspective we can appreciate the visual and emotional impacts of placing cultic installations on sacred mountains, or investing significance in groves of trees. These sacred places all linked together to form a wider and ideologically-laden space, and it was the duty of the Christians to destroy or convert these places, and reconfigure the broader sacred space.[5]

Re-conceptualising architectural space is a theme particularly associated with Christian Egypt; all over the country the newly enfranchised and dynamic Christian communities attacked the temples of the Pharaohs and built churches inside them. Such acts are heavily laden with rich symbolic meaning; we are seeing a shift in emphasis from the house of the god (the temple) to the idea of a more open, more democratic meeting place: the church (*ecclesia*) a place for the people, a more democratic and accessible space. Also, perhaps more prosaically, these vast structures offered scope for an easy conversion of space; it is, after all, much more economical to take over an existing large building than build a new one, but there is undeniably a symbolic meaning. Witness the crosses carved upon the hieroglyphic walls of the pharaonic temples at Philae, Denderah, Karnak and Medinet Habu, among others. This is not mere graffiti; it is a powerful statement of new ownership.

Once the place had been Christianised, then, on the larger scale, the reconceptualisation of the broader spatial canvas could be attempted. In the case of the West Bank of the Nile at Thebes, the process of reordering the pharaonic sacred landscape was accomplished by the mass settlement of new monasteries around the tombs and temples of the pharaohs.[6] The countryside – specifically the desert, abode of demons

28 A Christian altar and niche set up inside the Temple of Isis, Philae. *Niall Finneran*

– was the next challenge. The Christianisation of Egyptian rural space was accomplished through the actions of the determined and dynamic Christian hermits led by the famed St Antony and St Paul, although they may have tapped into a longer tradition of social memory. This domain of devils was acculturated, made holy, through the settlement of pious holy men and women seeking an escape from the temptations of earthly Alexandria, which was developing into a hotbed of Christian debate and tension mirroring wider political machinations. We have, at this point, rather got ahead of the narrative; let us then leave the Christian question, briefly, and consider the other side of the wider equation. What constituted the opposition to Christianity in Alexandria in late antiquity?

PAGAN VERSUS CHRISTIAN: THE INTELLECTUAL BATTLEGROUND

Even after the supposed triumph of Christianity within the Egyptian towns (although not yet in the countryside) 'paganism' remained socially and culturally highly important, especially among the urban elites. It is important again to emphasise that we cannot speak of a culturally or ideologically monolithic entity called 'paganism';[7] that much is clear from our consideration of the variety of Hellenistic and Roman ritual behaviour discussed in chapter two. Contemporary historical sources tell us of a wide variety of shrine forms within the city, a range of festivals and deities: Greek, Egyptian, Roman, oriental gods and goddesses and amalgamations thereof,[8] and each deity, it appears, was identified with a specific area of the city. In the harbour area for instance Poseidon, unsurprisingly, was a popular deity; Hellenic cults were celebrated in the Tychaion temple area, whilst in the Brucheion – at the centre of secular power within the city – dynastic cults were worshipped. The Serapeion maintained a paramount importance and Isis shrines (dedicated to the important Egyptian goddess) were scattered across the city.[9] This diversity of belief is reflected in the variety of personalities subsumed under the 'pagan' label; these cults mainly cut across all areas of society, but some personalities emerged, often in the field of intellectual endeavour and pagan philosophers were especially in demand as cultural icons.[10] The late antique city saw a reassertion of a very learned form of paganism, intellectually elevated, somewhat self-consciously nostalgic, harking back to perceived better days, and a philosophy that could be regarded as being very 'antiquarian' in character.[11] The Neoplatonist movement, which dominated the late antique city's elite intellectual fabric, also had a profound impact on the formation of a very dynamic, local Christian intellectual movement thus indicating the permeability of ideology and material culture within the city.

When one speaks of late 'pagan' survivals in Alexandria, it is the Neoplatonist philosophers that spring to mind. Based upon the ideals of learning nourished and developed in Ptolemaic Alexandria, the Neoplatonists unsurprisingly maintained a very syncretic and cosmopolitan outlook. Although overtly 'scientific', there was also room for more amorphous, supernatural beliefs based upon an idealised picture of Egypt's heritage. The role of the ancient Egyptian priest, for instance, resolved itself into the idea of a magician, somebody able to control the supernatural, a wise man (*magos*) who attracted much fascination among the Graeco-Roman cognoscenti in Egypt.[12] The School of Neoplatonism, the last fluorescence of this rich intellectual history of the city, was founded by Plotinus (205-70) in the mid-third century,[13] essentially during a period when Christianity was burgeoning amongst the urban population. Plotinus was generally very much against the use of magic and was hostile to the idea of *gnosis* (self-knowledge yielded by the revelation of God's wisdom), but some of his successors, such as Iamblichus and Proclus were not so unequivocal; the idea of Neoplatonism still carried a notion of self-knowledge attained through mystical and magical ways, although fundamentally the accent was upon the scientific method.[14] Plotinus' ideas definitely influenced the City's nascent Christian intellectuals such as Origen, who was particularly receptive to Platonist thinking regarding the nature of man's place in the Universe. Man need not be a passive spectator; he had it within him to know his destiny and attain perfection (a message at odds with prevalent Christian thinking, hence the idea of a gnostic heresy).[15]

The so-called Alexandrian school represented one of the hotbeds of early Christian thought in the Mediterranean world; Alexandria rivalled Antioch and Carthage as a centre for Christian debate and theological theory. The character of this School was very much a product of Alexandria's position as a centre of learning and enquiry; true to the cosmopolitan and syncretic nature of the city and its social life, the early Christian thinkers of Alexandria did not wholly ignore Plotinus' ideas. Let us briefly consider some of the key personalities who shaped Christian thought and learning in the city; such radical and rigorous thinkers as Origen, Clement and Athanasius were responsible for shaping Alexandria's distinctive identity as a Christian city, albeit one firmly rooted in the traditions of free enquiry nurtured by the Ptolemies, and continued by the Romans.

The Alexandrian Catechetical School produced a number of important Christian intellectuals. The founder, the great theologian Clement (*c.*150-215), was succeeded by the equally charismatic Origen (*c.*185-254), who produced a variety of works and translations including the Tetrapla (a translation of the Septuagint with commentaries by Origen set out in four parallel columns, the Hexapla which added the Hebrew text in both Hebrew and Greek characters and the Octapla which added translations from Jericho and Nicopolis),[16] and even though he was condemned after his death (owing to his ideas on the pre-existence of the human soul) he still retained an important place in the intellectual tradition of the early Church. Other luminaries included: Pantaenus (d. 195), Dionysios the Great (d. 264), and Didymus the Blind (310-398) who taught such famous figures as St Jerome and Rufinus, and who was credited with inventing an early form of Braille. We should also mention one of the truly charismatic figures of Christian Alexandria, Athanasius (295-373), a staunch opponent of the Arian heresy, who never failed to antagonise the Byzantine political and ecclesiastical authorities and whose *Life of St Antony* remains one of the most important sources for understanding the personality of the first Christian hermit (*colour plate 12*). If the Christian thinkers of Alexandria were prepared to admit a degree of pagan philosophy derived from the works of Plato, the Christian masses on the ground were not always so respectful of the pagan heritage. The intellectual battleground played out, now it was time to translate the struggle to the streets of the city itself.

PAGAN VERSUS CHRISTIAN: CONTESTED SPACES

It is clear is that, even as late as the fifth century, there was a vigorous and vocal high culture of 'paganism' in the city, but the presence of so many unbelievers was anathema to the newly powerful Christian authorities, and soon we begin to see the emergence of religious violence. After the Edict of Toleration in 313, relations between the new, burgeoning, dynamic Christian community and the elevated, higher-class 'pagans' were fraught. Conflict had always been a feature of Alexandrian urban space, but this ideological struggle had another element; a form of class warfare. In the words of one scholar, this was a case of pagan 'high culture' initially uneasily co-existing and then locked in combat with the 'low' culture of Alexandria's Christian community.[17] The narrative of this pagan/Christian struggle may be briefly outlined below.[18]

The conversion of the Temple of Kronos (Saturn) into a church at around 324 marks the beginning of the large-scale Christian appropriation of pagan ritual space. The violent Christian mobs rampaging across the city would have met little real opposition amongst the pagan groups, and given a tacit backing by the ecclesiastical authorities were almost regarded as being untouchable in the eyes of the law; indeed it was the monks from the rural monasteries who were often the most enthusiastic mob leaders. With the pagans lying low, the Christian mobs then took to fighting amongst themselves; in 339, for instance, they fought against the supporters of Athanasius. With the banning of sacrifices enacted in 341, and the conversion of the Caesareum into a church in 346, the Christians were beginning to remodel the city according to their own ideas, but it was not all one-way traffic: in 361 pagan rioters murdered George, the Arian Bishop of Cappadoccia. In 385 the Temples were officially closed, yet pagan power remained strong within certain urban centres; in 391, encouraged by Bishop Theophilos, a massive Christian mob attacked the Serapeion, which had been closed by Constantine in 325. The mob destroyed the pagan shrine there and established within its walls a monastic foundation and church dedicated to John the Baptist (they also removed the sacred Nilometer, thus severing the link with the ancient Egyptian gods). In addition, as if to sanctify the space further, a church dedicated to SS Cosmas and Damian was also instituted on the site, but its actual whereabouts remain unknown.

The church of John the Baptist was destroyed in 600, but restored under the Patriarch Isaac (681-84) whilst the city was under Muslim control. We hear nothing more of this church after the tenth century, but excavations of the Serapeion site in the late 1940s uncovered its ruins along with two shallow baptistery tanks, a cruciform tank for holy water and amphorae with Chi-Rho monograms carved onto their surfaces.[19] Other important pagan temples to fall into Christian hands at this time included the Tychaion and temple at Canopus, and then finally, in 399, came the Imperial order to destroy all rural temples, followed soon by the decree outlawing all urban temples. The Christianisation of Alexandria was almost complete.

The murder of the female pagan teacher Hypatia in 415 marked the end of Christian versus pagan conflict. The pagan city had essentially been all but eradicated, and a new Christian city grew in its place; a final triumph over paganism, however, did not guarantee peace. With no pagans to attack, Christian mobs turned upon the city's Jews or fought among themselves. In 414 for instance the Jews were ordered out of the city, whilst inter-Christian riots were common; those of 457, resulted in the murder of Bishop Proterius. If anything, the Christian triumph resulted in social anarchy across the city, but the physical topography had not changed irreversibly; in the words of one scholar 'the topog-

29 Indicative of a new order: Christian symbols upon the site of the archetypal place of pagan enjoyment, the Kom el-Dikka theatre. *Niall Finneran*

raphy of Alexandria was too contained by natural barriers to permit a reconfiguration of the pronounced design system'.[20] In short, although the Christians had stamped their identity on the pagan places, the wider urban space, a fixed Ptolemaic creation, did not overtly change. History has told us this much, but what (if any) is the key archaeological evidence for this ideological shift?

RECONSTRUCTING CHRISTIAN ALEXANDRIA: ARCHAEOLOGICAL APPROACHES

It was almost impossible physically (and perhaps economically) for instance, to construct new large-scale church buildings within the centre of the city itself; the main means of Christianising the urban space, as we have noted above, was the construction of the church building within pre-existing sacred sites. Soon the urban topography would be dominated centrally by places of worship, churches, and on the periphery of the city, by small, suburban monastic communities. Alexandria's fabric was studded with Christian buildings, many of them occupying sites of former pagan sacred significance.[21] This reuse of space worked on a number of levels, and often political motivations played a part. The church of the Blessed Virgin Mary built by St Theonas was sited strategically next to the Gate of the Moon and subsequently it became an Episcopal residence; it effectively controlled access to the city and dominated the approach (given this continuing theme of fluidity of meaning and syncretism of place it was subsequently converted into a mosque). The siting the church of St Michael in the Kronos temple was not just an action designed to take over a sacred space, more obviously it made a specific identification between the archangel Michael and the personality of Kronos himself. As the Greeks had borrowed and adapted native Egyptian deities (as subsequently did the Romans) so the earliest Christians were also able, to some small degree, to make a syncretism of sacred personality. So to return to the key methodological issue; what can archaeology tell us about the early Christian city? Can we account for the gradual assimilation of sacred places?

The form and location of the earliest church buildings in the city itself may only be traced by the study of textual sources, although in some cases we have wall paintings from domestic contexts in Kom el-Dikka that purport to show church architecture (see *30*). According to one source, 12 churches were definitely founded before the reign of Athanasius in the mid-late fourth century; some were foundations within pagan precincts, and others bore names of donor bishops.[22] Athanasius himself did not construct his so-called 'Great Church' – it was actually built just before his death in *c.*370, and this was sited upon the Temple of the Mendideion, and in turn it latterly became the Attarin mosque. Textual sources also tell us that Theophilus (385-412) was an enthusiastic church builder who according to tradition built a magnificent 'gold-covered church' which may possibly be the Church of Arcadius. In total, approximately 50 Christian buildings, which would include churches and martyria shrines, have been identified from contemporary accounts of Alexandria.[23] Martyria fulfilled different ritual roles than the parochial churches and were themselves often sited in localities where the martyrdom had taken place; in many cases there were a multitude of tombs dedicated to martyrs – this was especially the case with Mark, whose final resting place proved as elusive as that other key personality Alexander himself. Christian expansion and building was associated with a number of personalities; the Patriarch Theophilus, for instance, was an exceptional builder of churches, consecrating at least nine during his reign as patriarch (385-412), whilst other Patriarchs took little interest in forging a new Christian identity for the city. Political and national machinations also played a part in the shaping of Christian Alexandria and at this point we should consider some of the controversies that bedevilled the eastern Christian world in the mid-first millennium.

The aftermath of the church Council of Chalcedon in 451 effectively split the eastern Christian church. The background to the Chalcedonian debate is complex and is largely irrelevant to much of the current study, but a few facts need to be stated because as we shall see Alexandria would become the battleground for the competing political and religious groupings. Put simply, the Chalcedonian controversy focused upon different interpretations of the nature of Christ. An archimandrite named Eutyches (c.378-454) stated that Christ was at once human and divine (this viewpoint is mistakenly referred to as Monophysite; the labels Miaphysite or Henophysite are better used) and this perspective on the problem of how Christ should be viewed soon brought him into conflict with the church authorities and the Byzantine state. Eutyches' teachings were popular amongst the dynamic Christian thinkers of the near east and Africa, especially in Alexandria, but he was proclaimed heretical at the Council of Chalcedon, and all the key personalities who represented this view – from the Nile in Egypt to the Tigris in Persia – were anathematised by the Greek Church. In a sense, this was also a case of the political authorities of Byzantium flexing their muscles, but Eutyches' ideas were enthusiastically embraced by many Egyptians, indeed they largely reflected Alexandrian theology. The battle lines were being drawn: on one side the urban, Byzantine Greek-speaking orthodox clergy (known as Melkites, meaning people of the king, in mocking reference to their political affiliation) and on the other the Coptic-speaking Egyptian, predominantly rural and monastic supporters of Eutyche's now heretical views.

It should be noted that after the Chalcedonian schism 'ownership' of the churches of Alexandria varied according to the political situa-

Ten centimetres

30 This fresco from a house in the Kom el-Dikka area purports to show a late-antique church building. Redrawn from M. Rodziewicz (1984) *Alexandrie III: Les Habitations Romaines Tardives d'Alexandrie* (Warsaw: PWN) figure 247

tion, and their fortunes reflected the Melkite/Coptic schism. Executive patriarchal power was initially invested in the church of St Mark's martyrdom until the early fourth century when the Church of the Virgin Mary took on that role. The Coptic (i.e. anti-Chalcedonian) patriarchs were exiled from the city between 451 and 481 and in 539 when the Byzantine authorities, in a political act, established a Melkite see. Coptic power was vested in the outlying monastic establishments, although as we have seen on occasions the affiliation of these establishments was fluid.[24] It is not possible to recognise the affiliation of a church through architecture or decoration alone; Melkite Churches enjoyed extensive imperial patronage during the Byzantine period, and were thus probably larger, better appointed and located physically at the centre of the city. Coptic foundations probably existed more on the fringe of the city and real power was centred in the rural monasteries.

Moving away from the problem of identifying the ownership of Christian buildings in Alexandria, let us consider what is known, on the ground, about the Christian city from the mid-first millennium. The archaeological evidence presented in figure thirty one represents our best data for the archaeology of the late antique Christian city.

The textual evidence, however, suggests that there were many more church buildings in the city, and it shows up the relative lack of useful archaeological material. The following list is non-exhaustive, and is based upon an inventory from a late eleventh-century Arab account by Abu al-Makahrim.[25] The most important church in terms of the history of Egyptian Christianity, as it may have been Alexandria's first

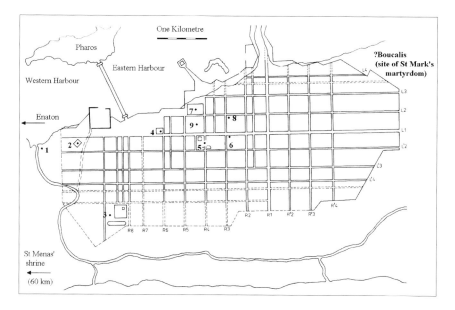

31 Key Christian sites in the late antique city. Compare with *11* noting reuse of pagan temple sites. Based upon B. Tkaczow (1990) 'Archaeological sources for the earliest churches in Alexandria' in W. Godlewski (ed.) *Coptic Studies: Proceedings of the Third International Conference of Coptic Studies 1984* (Warsaw: PWN) pp. 431-435 1. A small sepulchral chapel found in the Gabbari area, possible burial site of Bishop Peter, martyred in 311; 2. Possible site of the ninth-century 'Mosque of a thousand Pillars' which itself is presumed to be the site of Theonas' third-century church; two columns with distinctive Chi-Rho monograms were found in a nearby hospital garden (the mosque itself was demolished at the beginning of the nineteenth century); 3. The Serapeion site. Here two churches and monastery were built within the existing structure; 4. The Attarine mosque – built in 1084 and destroyed in 1830 – had possible reuse of architectural fragments from Athanasius' fourth-century church which must have stood near to the site; 5. The Kom el-Dikka suburb; frescoes and carvings of Christian subjects; 6. Possible site of Temple of Kronos (Saturn), converted in 326 into the church of Archangel Mikhael (also known as Bishop Alexander's church). Greek and Coptic inscriptions found nearby; 7. Site of Caesareum (converted into church in 324) and possible later Patriarchate building; 8. Identification of a site with an earlier Ptolemaic temple, possible site of St Theodore's church; 9. Forum area, site of St Sabas Church, the modern (1975) Greek Orthodox church, although the present (1975) church utilises much older architectural fragments (colour plate 13).

was St Mark's church, on the Boucalis – or the oxen pasture – which was hard by the site of his martyrdom on the seashore. We know from many textual sources that this church was destroyed by the Arabs during the course of their conquest in the seventh century, but in the spirit of good Muslim-Christian relations was thoroughly rebuilt by Patriarch Shenoute during the period 859-912. It was destroyed again, rebuilt again and finally destroyed in 1218. As a martyrium, it would have been an important place of pilgrimage, and ownership of the relics of the saint would have conferred a great deal of political and ideological power. We can assume that this place would have been the subject of extensive Melkite-Coptic rivalry, although after the Arab conquest it is probable (as was seen elsewhere where the Arabs deemed the Melkites to be too close to the Byzantine political authorities) that the church was given to the Copts, but the relics were taken by Venetian merchants in 828 to the church of San Marco in Venice, and this act created a massive ideological vacuum at the heart of the city.[26] No trace of this church survives, and it is probable that its foundations are probably now submerged under the waters of the eastern harbour.

The Great Church in the Caesareum (*Megale Ecclesia*), was the venue of Athanasius' conflict with the Arians, and he reconstituted the building in 368 with a dedication to St Michael. Again, this edifice represented a centre of political and religious power, and as such was continually disputed between Copts and Melkites prior to its destruction in 912. This church building is one of the earliest and most important foundations within the urban boundaries, but again little archaeological evidence for it survives, although it is possible that some evidence noted above may correspond to another of Athanasius' late-fourth-century foundations in the former Bendidion area, adjacent to the Attarine mosque. Another early foundation is the Church of Blessed Virgin Mary erected by St Theonas (282-300) on the edge of the Eunostos harbour; this church, according to historical records, was rebuilt and enlarged under Patriarch Alexander 313-28, and became known as St Mary's Cathedral until the end of fourth century, when the Great Church of St Michael in the Caesareum took over its role. The church was downgraded to a bishop's residence, then after the Arab conquest became the 'west mosque', subsequently known as the Mosque of a Thousand Columns.

Abu al-Makahrim mentions a number of other Christian foundations in Alexandria; in many cases the dating of their foundation and indeed

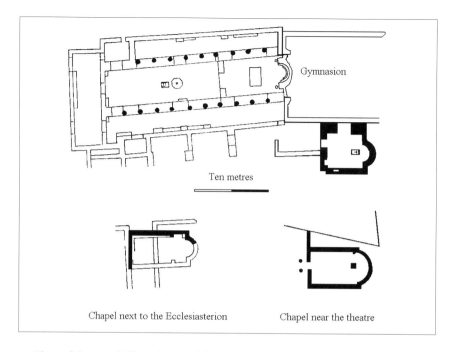

32 Plans of three probable ecclesiastical buildings within the Kom el-Dikka suburb. Top: chapel next to the gymnasium; bottom left: chapel next to the Ecclesiasterion; bottom right: chapel near the theatre. Redrawn from M. Rodziewicz (1984) *Alexandrie III: Les Habitations Romaines Tardives d'Alexandrie* (Warsaw: PWN) fig. 320

their actual location is problematic – other sources mention different names, and in many cases the identification of actual churches is duplicated. Combining Abu al-Makahrim's account and other sources we may recognise the following Christian places of worship (the number of churches would indicate a sizeable Christian population as late as the tenth century; some are clearly built upon earlier pagan shrines and others were subsequently converted into mosques). The following are noted as being some of the earliest extant churches: the Church of St Sabas (Mar Saba) was built into the Temple of Apollo (this presumably accords to the modern Greek Orthodox foundation); the Church of St John at Abu Kir mentioned as being a reliquary site; the Serapeion site with a church dedicated to St John the Baptist and Prophet Elijah, also known as Angleion and destroyed in the tenth century; the Church of St Theodore opposite the Serapeion; the Church of the Archangel Raphael on the Pharos island; a church dedicated to SS Cosmas and Damian

33 Fresco from House D, Street R4, Kom el-Dikka showing the Blessed Virgin and infant Christ. Redrawn from M. Rodziewicz (1984) *Alexandrie III: Les Habitations Romaines Tardives d'Alexandrie* (Warsaw: PWN) fig. 236

founded 284 in a stadium to the west of the colonnade on the main east–west street; the Church of Our Lady founded by the fifteenth Patriarch Maximus (264-82); the Church of the Archangel Mikhael in temple of Kronos; and the Church of the Emperor Arcadius (395-408). The following foundations are given as being established by Pope Christodoulus (1047-77, the sixty-sixth Patriarch): churches of St John the Evangelist, St Mercurius, Archangel Michael, St Menas and St George (and indeed other sources mention by name at least 24 other foundations variously described as being Coptic or Melkite).

In many cases the actual location of these churches is open to question, but it is noticeable that a number are explicitly stated to occupy sites of former pagan temples. It would also be useful, although beyond the scope of the present study, to attempt to chart the changing allegiances of the churches themselves. It would be hypothesised, for instance, that Melkite foundations and wealth would be gradually eroded after the Arab conquest. Although church buildings within the urban environment played an important part in the Christianisation of space in Alexandria, real executive power was vested in the monastic system. Although this is something we tend to associate with the countryside, monasteries played a very important role in the shaping of the Christian city itself.

The emergence of Christian monasticism in Egypt was one of the most important and far-reaching developments in the early Christian world. It is to Egypt that we should look when we consider the origins of Christian monasticism, a concept that soon spread rapidly into Syria and Palestine, Sudanese Nubia and Ethiopia, then with early Christian 'Nestorian' missionaries along the eastern trade routes of the Roman Empire into Mesopotamia and beyond, as well as into the sphere of the western Roman Empire and its political successors.[27] It was not an original idea to seek contemplative solitude on the periphery of society; Egypt had already witnessed charismatic movements in pre-Christian times – Philo had noted many so-called *therapeutae* (hermit healers) in the deserts around Alexandria,[28] and it is clear that the stark dichotomy between the earthly delights of the city and the contrasting harsh desert hinterlands was already engraved in the mindset of those citizens of Alexandria who wished to seek differing forms of spiritual inspiration.

In Egypt two parallel brands of Christian monastic organisation may be defined, and each were recast in varying degrees in the newly Christianised areas. The brand of solitary eremitic monasticism as popularly represented by St Antony was based upon complete withdrawal from the temptations of the city, where a single hermit or anchorite sought a life of solitude. The motivations for following this course of action were many and varied; many of the first Christian hermits tended to come from the more well-off strata of society, and in many cases the action of *anachoresis* (withdrawal) often had a more secular meaning: tax avoidance. These early charismatics drew heavily upon the Graeco-Roman magical tradition; whereas in Christian iconography the warrior cavalier saint was borrowed from Horus' iconography,[29] it also embodied a fundamental dualism, the fight between good and evil. The anchorites in the deserts saw their roles couched in traditional pre-Christian dualistic concepts, fights to the death with the demons of the desert.[30] It would be a mistake to see the anchorite as being a male loner; there were a number of famous female ascetics wandering the desert wastes around Alexandria and these are figures that have hitherto been rather marginalised by historians and archaeologists.

The potential for an archaeology of gendered religious space in and around Alexandria is immense; the British archaeologist Roberta Gilchrist has shown as much in a pioneering study of medieval nunneries in England;[31] we know from contemporary sources that Egyptian monasticism has provided a number of dynamic female ascetics and nuns[32] and it is clear that the space of the Alexandrian Christian hinterland was the domain of a number of peripatetic, perpetual pilgrims, many of them women. They inhabited the domain of demons; St Menas (of whom more later) was also commemorated alongside the female St Thecla who originated from Asia Minor. During late antiquity this pairing of the male and female saints was embodied in the iconography of ampullae – pilgrims' water flasks – when we begin to see the appearance of a recognisably Byzantine female alongside Saint Menas and his camels. Why should we begin to see this emphasis upon equality for female and male, both seen as equals within the pilgrim site of Abu Mina? It may well be that the ecclesiastical authorities recognised the important role played by women in the Egyptian Church, and as such developed a parallel, female-orientated pilgrim centre at Abu Mina;[33] this move to attract female pilgrims may be reflected in the construction of a double baptistery to the west of the martyr's church to cater for both sexes.

As a whole there is evidence of a progressive gendered space in the early Christian landscape; such a dichotomy would naturally be reinforced during Islamic times. We know about individual figures, the ascetics, male and female, but there was another important form of monasticism developing beyond the urban boundaries of Alexandria and down along the Nile Valley. The other main type of monasticism in late antique Egypt grew from the idea of the *Lavra*, the loose and free agglomeration of monks and their dwellings crowded around a central charismatic figure. The communal (coenobitic) system was developed, according to Egyptian historical sources, by St Pachomius (Pachome) and subsequently was refined by his successor Shenouda.[34] This monastic way of life demanded poverty and obedience, settlement within a community and also emphasised work as well as contemplation – Pachomian monasteries were essentially independent, self-sufficient quasi-villages. This Egyptian monastic archetype soon found favour rapidly elsewhere; in Syria, for instance, the ascetic or holy man did not tend to withdraw from society like his Egyptian counterpart, but took on the role of a local political mediator,[35] and here the dichotomy between the desert and sown was enhanced in a different setting: for the Syrians the mountains became the desert and the place for withdrawal, or in the case of St Simeon Stylites withdrawal was attained through sitting atop a pillar. The Egyptian form of communal monasticism soon found its way, via John Cassian, into western Europe, where during the fourth century at Marseilles, a monastic community structured along Egyptian lines was founded.[36] In any case, monasticism was essential to the growth and development of the church in many areas, not just in Egypt. The monastic system also supported and nourished the urban Christianity burgeoning in Alexandria; this raw dichotomy between desert and sown, town and country, nature and culture is actually more permeable than has hitherto been recognised.

Monasteries did not necessarily have to be located in the desert wastes; there is plenty of evidence of a form of city-based monasticism that was very popular elsewhere among the urban elites in the late antique world.[37] We can see a similar picture in Alexandria, although in the words of one scholar 'their distinct locations limited their impact upon the Christianisation of Alexandrian urban design';[38] in short, monasteries in Alexandria were too physically peripheral. Possible evidence for one of these urban monasteries may be found in the Kom el-Dikka site; the so-called House D on Street R4 has yielded a number of exceptionally fine Christian frescoes and the associated agglomeration of buildings could indicate that this site was a monastery.[39] The paintings include pictures of Christ, the Virgin Mary and child as well as assorted pieces of graffiti which indicate a clear Christian sympathy of the writer,[40] and some designs clearly show church architecture (see *30*). Special interest attaches to a distinctive three-pronged cross motif (*34*); this design is clearly similar to certain modern Ethiopian Orthodox crosses, and it may be making a statement about the debate over the nature of Christ as reflected in the struggles at the Council of Chalcedon. Wider liturgical and political debates, then, may be reflected in the domestic material culture of the city;[41] this is an unusual and potentially compelling piece of evidence for the vigorous ground-swell of anti-Chalcedonian feeling in what was still essentially a Byzantine urban space.

There is also evidence for other larger monasteries within the vicinity of the city. To the northeast of Alexandria (probably at Canopus)

34 Tripartite cross found on the walls of House D, Street R4, Kom el-Dikka. Redrawn after M. Rodziewicz (1984) *Alexandrie III: Les Habitations Romaines Tardives d'Alexandrie* (Warsaw: PWN) fig. 242

was the large *Metanoia* monastic settlement, which may be identified as being the Dayr Qibriyus, an important Melkite foundation.[42] To the east of the city walls, roughly by the new library site by the Corniche, and marking the area of St Mark's martyrdom on the oxen pasture, was the extensive church-monastery of St Mark (or the Dayr Asfal al-Ard).[43] This was an extensive monastery and it held the important relics of St Sophia. Just as church foundations switched allegiance reflecting wider political and ecclesiastical developments, so did the monasteries within the close vicinity of the city (it must be emphasised that many of the rural monasteries and the upper Egyptian foundations did remain, by and large, resolutely anti-Chalcedonian); after the Council of Chalcedon this monastery became Melkite and was destroyed during the Arab conquest.[44] An additional monastic settlement was probably located in the Brucheum quarter, and the monastery of the Tabennesiotes was sited within the Serapeion in the southeastern quarter of the city.

Of these urban monasteries, mentioned widely in varied historical sources, little is known and it is unlikely that archaeologists will be able to discover their true whereabouts. It is broadly recognised by modern scholars, however, that during the fourth century there were extensive suburban monastic settlements divided almost equally between the Melkite orthodox and Coptic groups – the writer Palladius mentions some 2000 individual monastic units in and around the city, a truly large figure that must take into account individual hermitages;[45] monks tended self-consciously to adopt more marginal places in the city, perhaps abandoned suburbs, which were places more redolent of the desert, places to find solitude away from the busier areas of central Alexandria,[46] but it is possible that these urban monks actually represent a distinct ascetic class apart. St Jerome, writing in 380, makes three distinctions of monks: hermits and cenobites (whom we have already met) and the debauched remnuoth, who were urban apostates (he may actually be referring to the apoptactic movement).[47] It is entirely possible that some of these urban hermits were not entirely given over to a life of contemplation and prayer and refused to renounce the relative comfort of the suburbs for the bourgeoning semi-anchoritic communities of the deserts to the south on Mount Nitria, Kellia and the Scetis Desert. This reluctance to move into the harsher, more demanding ascetic worlds may have been a reason why such people should have been regarded as being so despicable. They could not be proper monks whilst they lived on the suburban margins of one of the most exciting and dynamic cities in the world.

Monastic power in the Alexandrian region was not, then, focused upon the city itself; it is rather westwards – along the Taenia Ridge that formed the northern edge of Lake Mareotis and a barrier between the sea – that we must look for evidence of intensive monastic settlement, where according to one authority 'nascent Monophysite resistance (to the Chalcedonian Melkites) centred upon the numerous and wealthy monasteries.[48] If the city predominantly reflected the Greek-speaking, heavily Byzantine, pro-Chalcedonian ascendancy, then the countryside beyond the city walls was truly the realm of the fiercely anti-Chalcedonian Egyptian monks, dynamic ascetics who readily took up leadership of the rampaging Christian mobs within the city. It is almost as if the old Ptolemaic dichotomy of urban: rural; Greek: Egyptian was being reproduced.[49] Again, the following outline of this anti-Chalcedonian centre of power is based upon textual accounts; no intensive archaeological survey of this region has been attempted, and such a study would surely contribute to the debate surrounding the nature of political and ecclesiastical power in Alexandria prior to the victory of Islam in the seventh century.

The first key monastic site to be encountered outside of Alexandria upon the ridge was the Lithazomenon (or monastery of 40 saints) and

St Peter's Bridge. Described by the famous writer John Moschos in the sixth century as being two monasteries near a water course (which water course is not known, although it must be linked to the canal system that joined Lake Mareotis to the sea), and being important as the residence of Patriarch Peter 1st (300-11).[50] We may assume that this building was located adjacent to the western city gate and it is therefore likely that this site has since been covered over by urban development since the nineteenth century.[51] At the fifth milestone westwards from the Gate of the Moon was the monastery of Pempton, marking the true beginning of the Taenia monastic group, which was a zone also labelled the *Eremika*, meaning the desert by the sea during late antiquity. John Moschos tells us that this area was the home of the city gallows and that a temple dedicated to Kronos was also located nearby (again urban encroachment in the area has probably covered over the remains of this monastery).

At the ninth milestone from gate was the highly important and extensive monastic complex of the Enaton (also known in Arabic as Deir az-Zujaj or the monastery of glass). Some writers [52] have suggested that its location should be identified with the modern village of Dikhayleh, where some archaeological material, only vaguely described as being possibly Christian has been noted, but this village is too close to Alexandria, and if anything the site of the Pempton should accord with Dikhayleh. The Enaton was located, according to sources, in a fertile agricultural zone with its own dedicated anchorage on Lake Mareotis, and was an important stop on the pilgrimage route to Abu Mina (discussed below). The Enaton was really more than a large monastery with cloister; the settlement comprised a number of autonomous monastic *laurae* (semi-independent, semi-cenobitic agglomerations of individual hermitages) and Pachomian settlements proper, each linked explicitly to the identity of a founder father or *Hegoumenos*. In a sense this could be described as being a 'federal' institution and it attracted monks from far afield (especially Palestine) becoming noted as an important intellectual centre. The Enaton was the centre of anti-Chalcedonian power; the Coptic Patriarch resided here, symbolically beyond the bounds of the city walls and its large orthodox population. In a sense this major political and liturgical schism was mirrored in the location of the key centres of each church, an urban-rural dichotomy was clear to see, with the Copts relegated to the periphery of the urban socio-economic system.[53] The fate of this large and truly important monastic centre is unknown; it began to decline after the Islamic conquest in the seventh century, and its downfall may have been hastened by climatic deterioration,[54] although this is not clear in the regional environmental-history sequence, and it is of course unlikely that a monocausal factor such as this should be invoked to explain away an important event in a highly complex socio-economic and historic context.

The site features in the fourteenth-century records of Abu Salih the Armenian, where the Arab traveller Al Makrizi notes:

> It stands outside Alexandria, and is also called Al Habatun, and bears the name of St George the Great. Formerly it was the custom of the Patriarchs at their election to betake themselves from the Mu'allakha at Misr (the 'Hanging Church' in Cairo) to the monastery of Az-Zajaj, but this is not now done.[55]

The monastery's name was still mentioned on western maps into the fifteenth century, but by then was probably a mere toponym rather than a group of buildings. How and why such a huge agglomeration of Christian settlements, of obvious wealth and importance, should disappear so thoroughly is one of the potential great unanswered historical and archaeological questions for scholars of Egypt's medieval period.

At the 18th milestone west of the city gate was the Oktokaidekaton monastery which was mentioned in the *Life of St Theodora* as a desert place with pleasant irrigated gardens and harbour; John Moschos noted that it was structured along the same lines as the Enaton, so rather than a single monastic entity we should perhaps visualise an agglomeration of *laurae* and Pachomian settlements.[56] Finally, at the 20th milestone was the monastery of the Eikoston – or Kalamon.[57] Again, although these sites are mentioned by dependable historical sources, none have been located by archaeologists. It is clear that this 20-mile stretch of land was the home of a large number of varied and semi-autonomous monastic communities, and a number of historical sources stress their importance and wealth, and that of the church in and around the city as a whole.[58] It seems, however, that these monasteries just disappeared for reasons unknown, and have not since been located apart from random reports of vague finds around villages on the Taenia.[59] This more local monastic picture should be situated within the wider regional context; important clusters of monasteries could also be found at Nitria,[60] to the south of the Mareotis region, and further southwards still at Kellia, and finally and most importantly the cluster around the Wadi Natrun, the Scetis desert of antiquity.[61] These communities formed a large and influential monastic power bloc at the core of the power base of the Egyptian Christian church and archaeologists have only recently begun to look at the question of their relationships within the wider ecclesiastical system.

As a whole the system of monasticism played little part in the Christianisation of Alexandria's space, but it did play a very important role in the Christianisation of the rural landscape; although urban ascetics and monastic houses clearly did exist (often we find hermits living in suburban cemeteries) it is clear that the real power lay with the rural ascetics:'city and hinterland played off one another in late antique Egypt to a degree perhaps unparalleled in the rest of the Empire'.[62] Whereas the church building often represented the Christianisation of a single place, a locus, the monastery was part of a wider scheme of a Christianisation of *space*; they tamed and domesticated the desert zones. Another important social and ideological factor assisted in the consolidation of the Christian space. Martyria physically situated the remains of a revered and holy personality within a discrete area, forming a shrine, a place to visit. Within the urban zone the remains of St Mark fixed Christian identity and provided a focus of pilgrimage, but Alexandria was also at the centre of a much wider regional pilgrim landscape.

CHRISTIAN PILGRIMAGE, URBAN SPACE AND LANDSCAPE

In the early Christian Church – and of course not just in Egypt – the act of pilgrimage was one of the most important parts of the ritual cycle of life. This process demanded not just a physical journey to seek out the remains and shrine of a particularly devout saint; the act of travel followed in many cases a 'preset' ritual landscape, one moved along a prescribed set of places and in a sense the journey itself was as important as the ultimate destination. Before considering the specific context of pilgrimage in and around Alexandrian urban space in late antiquity, we need to look a little deeper at the idea of pilgrimage in history. The idea of pilgrimage embodies a number of key themes and is as much of a psychological journey as a physical one.[63] The placing of relics of a particularly devout saint within a landscape acted as a centralising social force, part and parcel of the process of Christianisation of space discussed earlier in this chapter, and formed on the larger scale the focal point of a sacred geography. The end of this ritual movement, the ultimate goal of the pilgrimage, need not have been a martyrium, or tomb, a dead individual; early Christian Egyptian landscapes, deserts, were home to a variety of charismatic holy individuals, and as their fame grew as teachers and spiritual directors, so too they became in their own right a centre of living pilgrimage.[64]

We have seen in chapter one how Alexandria became a centre of a kind of pilgrimage during the Hellenistic and Roman years; people came to seek out learning as well as visiting the city's shrines and temples. Indeed the idea of pilgrimage was also well known in pharaonic times in Egypt.[65] The large Jewish population of Alexandria and Egypt as a whole also engaged in extensive peregrinations; within Egypt the ritual complex at Elephantine Island near Aswan was a favoured destination and for those with wealth and influence the ultimate goal was the Temple of Jerusalem or Mount Sinai – where Moses was presented with the Ten Commandments – whilst smaller-scale pilgrimage sought out the tombs of dead heroes and ancestors.[66] It is tempting to see a kind of link between this idea of pilgrimage and veneration of ancestors, a cult of the dead among the Jews and the later Christian cult of the saints, a means of tapping into a shared social memory.

The sacred geography of the Christian pilgrim's landscape – the space – is held together by a network of sacred places: the key pilgrimage centres. This dynamic between the space and place, an important theme in our study, has been described thus: 'if space allows movement, place is pause'.[67] The relevance to the idea of pilgrimage emphasises the equal importance of the movement, the journey itself. In and around Alexandria there are a number of significant places of Christian pilgrimage, but one place arguably has had the most influence upon the shaping of the city as an international place in late antiquity. Approximately 45km (c.28 miles) to the south-west of Alexandria, in the desert wastes of Mareotis, we find one of the most important regional Christian pilgrim centres: the site of Abu Mina (its modern Arabic name). The fame of this centre, which commemorates the martyrdom of St Menas, spread far beyond Egypt's borders in late antiquity. Devout pilgrims from all over the Roman Empire came to pay homage to one of the most important saints of the early Church. This was

35 View across the late antique pilgrim centre of Abu Mina in 2002. The site is at risk from a rising water table. *Sarah Finneran*

clearly a site of international importance and its very existence, both ideological and socio-economic, was dependent upon its relationship with Alexandria itself.

The development of this pilgrim centre has been revealed through over a century of archaeological work here,[68] and its importance is preserved today in the form of a large and modern Coptic monastery on the site. The earliest excavator, a German archaeologist named Kaufmann, was able to show that the earliest tomb complex was sited within a pagan hypogeum tomb and the presence of associated small monkey statuettes and Horus-Harpocrates stelae would suggest that this may have been in earlier times a Graeco-Roman sanctuary of some form. As the importance of the place grew, so it developed: the simple mausoleum complex was rapidly superseded by a fifth-century church and latterly a large basilica. By the end of the fifth century, a great basilica had been added to the east of this structure and in the sixth century, probably during the reign of the Byzantine Emperor Justinian, a martyrs' church was built.

Reflecting the secular concerns of a pilgrimage space, we see the development of distinctive rest houses/guest houses (*xenodochia*), a palace area for the Hegoumenos (the head of the community) and analysis of tombs within the large cemetery area clearly shows that this became a fashionable area for the burial of elite Alexandrian families. Such was the popularity of this site that a purpose-built port complex was constructed on Lake Mareotis at Philoxenite on the orders of Emperor Anastasius (491–518) to cater for the annual large influx of pilgrims who came from all over the Roman world; distinctive clay flasks stamped with a depiction of St Menas which were used by pilgrims to bring home holy water or oil from the sacred site have been found all over central Europe, attesting to the very international outlook of Alexandria and its hinterland in late antiquity.[69]

The socio-economic aspect of the pilgrimage dynamic aside, the biography of Abu Mina also reflects the ongoing post-Chalcedonian struggles among the Christians of Alexandria. Just as the Taenia ridge and Enaton (beyond the gates of the city) had become a refuge for the disenfranchised Copts and a centre for their power, it was also the case that such an important economic and religious centre should have to be kept in the hands of the pro-Chalcedonian Melkites. The only concession to the Copts was the construction – at a safe and insulating distance from the core of the site – of the so-called North Basilica. Again, the biography of a sacred place reveals more than the concerns of ritual: it mirrors wider political developments. Ostensibly a place for reflective pilgrimage, the site was also at the centre of a bitter political power struggle.

We have already outlined the difficulties inherent in using archaeology alone to differentiate between the conflicting Christian groups; often it is the physical isolation of a church or monastic complex that reflects the isolation (at the politico-religious level) of the populist Copts. The use of space within the North Basilica would, however, appear to reflect Coptic liturgy, especially in the use of three altars (the prohibitions of Gregor of Nyssa in the fourth century who stated that an altar may be only used for a mass once a day) and a distinctive return aisle on the western side of the church interior, behind the narthex, or vestibule. With the Arab Conquest, however, it was the Copts who now found favour with the new masters. The mainly pro-Byzantine, pro-Chalcedonian, Melkites were disenfranchised and subsequently Abu Mina became an important pilgrimage centre for the Copts, although its importance had waned by the twelfth century. In a sense, the spiritual centre of the community lost its importance with the removal in the thirteenth century of the saint's bones to Cairo, but even earlier

36 The importance of memory of place. The modern monastery at Abu Mina. *Sarah Finneran*

the rich marble of the church had been plundered in 836 on the orders of a certain Al Mu'Tasim to build his grand palace in Samaria,[70] and it would have been inevitable that soon the desert would reclaim the site, which lay undisturbed until its rediscovery in 1905. More than any other Christian site in Egypt, Abu Mina tells us much about the political and secular concerns that underpinned the solemn ritual conducted around the bones of the saint.

Abu Mina is not the only Christian pilgrimage site within the environs of Alexandria. At the other end of the Alexandrian landscape we find the Shrine of SS Cyrus and John at Menouthis, which, although probably not as large as Abu Mina, was undoubtedly as important. Situated approximately 19km (*c.* 12 miles) to the east of Alexandria, roughly in the area of modern Abu Kir, this shrine, along with Abu Mina, formed one of the key sacred places in the wider, regional Christian sacred landscape.[71] Nothing remains of the shrine today, but during the sixth and seventh centuries this was one of the most popular pilgrim destinations in the area, the centre of a healing cult and the shrines of the two martyrs of Diocletian's persecutions. Again, as with many of the holy spaces we have considered thus far, the ideological meanings of the place are complex and multivocal: Menouthis was the site of a vigorous Isis cult, and acquired considerable importance in Graeco-Roman times; the place then became a centre for Christian veneration, although prior to 489, the Isis cult continued to flourish alongside Christianity.

In common with many Christian places, ownership and control of the shrine became disputed after the rift caused by Chalcedon; undoubtedly, given the quality of the shrine's sculpture on display in the Graeco-Roman Museum in Alexandria, this was a highly important site and ownership or control over it would have been desired. During the sixth century it is clear that the main shrine at Abu Mina was under the control of the pro-Chalcedonian Melkites, but the affiliation of this shrine is unknown; Coptic written sources make no mention of it, so we must assume that in a sense it had been 'written out' of history. Like the other major pilgrim centre at Abu Mina, it is clear that pro-Chalcedonian Greek hegemony over the sacred places within the regional sacred Christian space was assured – at least up until the Arab conquest in the seventh century. We have considered what constitutes Christian place and space in late antique Alexandria and have seen how these places and spaces were recast in the light of new ideological schemes, both pagan versus Christian and inter-Christian rivalry. This form of syncretism is also reflected, we have seen, in the intellectual underpinning of the distinct brand of Alexandrian Christianity. Remaining with this theme of cosmopolitanism and eclecticism, let us finally consider here how the Christians of Alexandria viewed their afterlife.

THE CHRISTIANISATION OF DEATH

In the last chapter we considered the nature of death and burial in Hellenistic and Roman Alexandria, making the important point that funerary archaeology can tell us a great deal about society and ideology in general. The Christianisation of burial practice is an important theme which highlights issues of syncretism. Whilst the non-Christian burial space was delimited in the *necropoleis*, to the Christian the place of death was where one awaited resurrection; to this end there were dedicated Christian burial zones: *Koimeteria*, the cemetery.[72] In many cases, reuse of existing tombs was the primary theme of Christian burial in late antique Alexandria; a Christianisation of space for the dead is evidenced, for instance, at the Gabbari catacombs where we find crosses scratched on the loculus walls and bodies are often laid out with the ubiquitous pilgrimage souvenirs of the region: the Menas ampullae.[73]

Cemeteries sprung up around the popular pilgrimage centres too; the desire to be buried close to a martyr or saint (*ad Sanctos*) meant that large dedicated cemetery areas sprung up on the fringes of the pilgrim city at Abu Mina and also among the anchoritic settlements of Kellia to the south of Alexandria. Here, vicariously, wealthy urban Christians were physically transported beyond the bounds of the city and placed within the sanctified desert to enjoy the proximity and reflected glory of being buried next to a famed martyr or monk; such themes are common all over the late antique world. We have already noted in connection with the Ptolemaic and Roman city of the dead that by and large Christians were not cremated, the treatment of the body was like that of the earlier Egyptians: they were laid out.

Analysis of the decorative attributes of high-status Christian tombs of this period bears witness to a degree of syncretic borrowing of non-Christian motifs. Friezes were popular in the catacombs and they did not show scenes from the Bible; rather traditional pagan hunting scenes, with an emphasis on the natural world.[74] Grave markers appeared in a variety of forms: *stelae*, varied shapes of cross with funerary invocations and niches set within for food offerings for the dead (again another non-Christian survival) are all noted and many 'pagan' nature motifs are also used as decorative devices, peacocks being especially popular. There was, then, no Christian simplicity about these grave markers and tomb constructions, they still embodied any number of non-Christian artistic and symbolic motifs. The role of the artisan was also very important; carving and tomb decoration was a popular trade and skilful carvers were much in demand. Any analysis of the corpus of their works has tended to draw an artificial dichotomy between Hellenistic and Coptic styles; in common with the cosmopolitan nature of the city over time we cannot pigeonhole in such a simplistic manner; there are many differing shades and nuances of artistic style, and it is even possible to speak of different regional schools of funerary sculpture and embellishment,[75] but on the whole Christian funerary liturgy emphasised the idea of community, a common bond in death, and it is therefore not surprising that there is little scope for great variation in Christian burial practice. Such a theme is certainly indicated by the relative decline of the funerary portrait which attested to the wealth and status of the deceased.[76] In addition it also seems that the funerary inscriptions incorporated a degree of pagan structure and style.[77] These, then, are the material and intellectual manifestations of Christianity upon Alexandria. Without doubt these were profound cultural and ideological developments that clearly impacted upon urban and rural place and space in and around the city itself, but the impact of Christianity should not be thought of, in this case at least, as being a spiritual or cultural phenomenon; there were other far-reaching implications. The new-found power of the Church within Alexandria saw a redefinition of the city's economic system.

THE SOCIO-ECONOMICS OF CHRISTIANITY

During the sixth century, the role and power of the patriarch took on a more secular aspect, especially that of the Melkite Patriarch, who was politically close to the imperial power base of Constantinople.[78] The Patriarch, apart from overseeing the spiritual wellbeing of Alexandria's citizens, also was responsible for the political and economic control of the city. The Church was at the centre of much of the trade in northern Egypt; the Churches (both Coptic and Melkite) possessed extensive fleets of maritime and riverine boats and the textile and grain trade formed the core of the economic trade network (even as far as western Britain where the tin trade with Cornwall was clearly vital)[79] as is witnessed by the extensive archives from the Episcopal Palace in Alexandria. Egypt also shipped massive amounts of grain to Constantinople,[80] thus retaining its role of the granary of the Empire that it had held in Roman times. The churches controlled many aspects of trade and currency in the city and in many cases records show us that they were actively engaged in money lending.

On the whole the economic base of the Byzantine city was fundamentally the same as the Ptolemaic and Roman city; we can only guess at this as legal records written on perishable papyrus – which are so numerous elsewhere in Egypt at this time – are completely lacking for Alexandria.[81] What we can tell, at least, is that the Marea region especially was highly fertile, and in every sense provided the agricultural, economic powerhouse for the late Antique city. Perhaps the most obvious pattern of economic change in the late antique period in Egypt as a whole, and one which certainly reflects the growing importance of Christian Alexandria on the Mediterranean stage, is the shift from the traditional, African, Egyptian agricultural economy of seed oil cultivation and beer making to the Mediterranean economy based upon olive oil and viticulture, a pattern that had begun to emerge in Ptolemaic times.[82]

It is clear that during the mid-fourth century, at a time when Christianity had attained official recognition in the city, the Church itself held little wealth (manifested in land holdings); this is clear from a text called the Hermopolite land register,[83] but soon the Patriarchal church at Alexandria began to acquire extensive land holdings and with these holdings came a great degree of socio-political as well as economic influence. The Church began to take an interest in controlling the maritime trade, for here was an opportunity for immense wealth creation potential and attainment of prestige. From Leontius' *Life of the Patriarch John the Almoner* (612-7) we know that the bishop had the power to withhold land taxes and disrupt shipping; the Patriarch had his own fleet of ships and the church wealth holdings were administered by dedicated stewards or *oikonomi*. Before the Arab conquest, then, the Church had attained a massive degree of socio-economic, political and naturally ideological power;[84] it had built from small beginnings and although prone to periods of violent internecine conflict, shaped the secular face of the city in response to a gradual weakening of political direction from Constantinople.

Christianity did not 'triumph', there was no mass popular conversion to a new and monolithic ideology,[85] but the social and symbolic space of the city was recast; 'pagan' ideas survived, as is witnessed by the continuing popularity of the Isis Temple at Menouthis well into the fifth century. The original Nile-centred cults survived in a new form more acceptable to Christians, old concepts such as patronage, craft guilds and healing cults survived.[86] The Christians of Alexandria, urban and predominantly well educated, did not forget or deny their Hellenistic heritage. In this most cosmopolitan of late antique cities, cultural, social and religious syncretism remained a key theme. Cosmas Indicopleustes – the author of the sixth-century treatise on the contemporary Christian world (The *Christian Topography*, the original of which is in the Vatican library) – displayed, in the words of one scholar 'a purely Hellenistic erudition',[87]

Neoplatonist ideas permeate the writings of the early Christian thinkers and the earliest Christian art and manuscript illustration in Egypt and its neighbours show a number of obvious conventions that may be attributed to the Hellenistic aesthetic.

'Christianisation', worked on a number of levels, not solely the ideological. We have investigated the idea of syncretism of space, how Christianity reconceptualised and adapted sacred spaces; we have seen how cultural and artistic motifs were retained in a Christian setting, we have seen too how personalities could be Christianised, such as the link between Michael and Kronos, and also we may speak of a Christianisation of time, such as the appropriation and re-conceptualisation of pre-Christian festivals.[88] But the next chapter in the urban biography of Alexandria sees a shattering collapse of the certainties of the Roman world and the arrival, from the deserts of the east, of a new religion and a new way of life. Perhaps more than any other cosmological outlook the advent of Islam radically changed the nature of Alexandria forever.

four

ISLAMIC ALEXANDRIA AND BEYOND

The arrival of the Arab armies in Egypt during the mid-seventh century shocked the city from its comfortable existence as a major settlement of the now diminishing Byzantine Empire. Whilst the Muslim conquest of Alexandria saw a far-reaching socio-economic and ideological reorganisation of urban space, it also marked importantly an erosion of Alexandria's role as an important political centre; perhaps the most profound development was the removal of secular governmental power away from Alexandria to the new settlement at Fustat – on the site of modern Cairo. The reasons for this desire to move from Alexandria are complex, but it is probable that the new Arab overlords wished to make a clean break with the past. Alexandria, as a planted urban space with rigid planned zones did not fit, as we shall see, with the idealised and free Arab 'city', and in any case the place was full of alien ideological remembrances.[1]

After the Muslim conquest Alexandria retained an ideological importance for the Christian Church. In terms of population make up, numbers and indeed that amorphous quality of 'social memory', it was still effectively a Christian city, both in the ideological and political spheres. Political leadership was still largely vested in the Melkite, Orthodox ecclesiastical authorities, with their links to Byzantine power over the waters of the eastern Mediterranean at Constantinople, but this status would soon be eroded. With the collapse of the Byzantine system there was an immediate power vacuum; there was effectively no formal secular framework for governance, so the Church fulfilled this role. In time, the Arab authorities recognised that the secular power of the Church could not continue to prop up civil administration, and a governor – in the first instances a Christian – would be appointed to oversee the governance of the city.[2] In a sense then there was no revolutionary, overnight change in the day-to-day life of Alexandria's citizens (a situation mirrored on the wider Egyptian scale; one might add that the great Christian cities of the east, such as Jerusalem and Antioch, also maintained a distinct Christian identity for hundreds of years to come).

The process of the reconceptualisation of urban space in Alexandria during late antique times – which began during the first flush of emergent Christian power and was hastened by the Arab conquest – was only part of a much wider series of changes affecting the large urban centres of the western and eastern old Roman world. All through the old Roman Empire of the west, and the New Rome centred upon Constantinople, the certainties of the design of urban space, ordered and symmetrical, were fast disappearing. Put simply – and as a generalisation – we are seeing, in this post-classical world, the transformation of the role of the urban elites, moving away from power vested in an aristocracy to a more meritocratic perspective. The wholesale construction of new fortified spaces within cities (the *poleis* of the east) reflected these new sociopolitical uncertainties, with more emphasis upon the role of the church in the city and the emergence of a new economically powerful, mercantile class. These processes are also reflected in the early Arab towns with the emergence of the *suq*, which reconfigured the role of the Forum and the colonnaded roads in the former Roman towns of the Levant and north Africa into a less formalised urban space reminiscent of the great eastern bazaars. It is worth emphasising the fact again that urban change in Egypt was part of a much wider phenomenon and is not solely attributable to the arrival of Islam.[3]

What was the immediate impact of the Arab conquest and more specifically of Islam upon the urban space of Alexandria? First, let us be clear about the opportunities afforded by archaeology alone for recognising this important cosmological shift. We cannot simply isolate a series of diagnostic traits (such as burial typologies, buildings of worship, etc.) that allow us to make a clear judgement upon religious affiliation. We must be cautious about the nature of the evidence. The work of the British archaeologist Timothy Insoll has alerted us to the potential archaeological visibility of Islam; he counsels against the idea that Islam is a monolithic entity both culturally and ideologically speaking (just as there is no single brand of paganism, Judaism or even Christianity). We can infer the presence of Muslim communities from mosques, burial evidence, even dietary remains and, most importantly for this study, the wider community environment: the Islamic town.[4] The problem comes with trying to tease out syncretic influences and understand local cultural idiosyncrasies.

What do we understand by the idea of Islamic town planning? Firstly, and again coming back to ideas of syncretism of place and space, it is highly difficult to differentiate an early, pristine and purely Islamic town within the area of the Byzantine Empire. Many so-called 'original' Islamic settlements in the Levant, for example, are often built upon Roman or Byzantine settlements and thus adapted the spatial configurations of the classical or post-classical city – this is true of the major cities such as Damascus and Aleppo. They are undoubtedly important Islamic towns, but were based upon a Roman template. Excavations on complex sites in late pre-Islamic Arabia have proved only that settlements there are too small to be meaningfully described as being cities, and in any case the preferred Arab form of community (*Medina*) during the period of Mohammed's conquests was the tented military encampment, the *Amsar*, which, although notionally peripatetic, conformed to a basic structure wherein the central focus was upon a Friday mosque and governor's residence (*dar al-Imara*).[5] As a rule then early Islamic urban patterns conform to the underlying structure of the classical city, although there is a trend to the narrowing of streets (chariots are no longer the vehicle of choice, it is now the donkey and cart or line of camels) and, as noted earlier, we see a shift of economic emphasis to craft and mercantile activity at the centre of the urban unit: this is best represented by the *suq* or bazaar. Ideological focus naturally centred upon the mosque (the *Jami* mosque was specifically used for Friday prayers) and political and social power was vested in the citadel and palace (*Casbah*). Additional elements of Arab towns included hospitals (*maristan*), religious schools (*madrashas*) and the ubiquitous bathhouse (*hamman*) complex (the latter is probably a derivation from the Roman bath). Internally one would recognise discrete suburbs (*rabat*) based upon residence for different ethnic groups and the city would be surrounded by a wall, with burials taking place beyond the city limits. The site of 'Anjar – an Umayyad site half-way between Beirut (Berytus) and Damascus – is a very good example of an early Islamic urban form, a precursor of the ordered symmetrical town planning of the Abbasids such as we find in Baghdad, a rare example of an almost pristine Islamic settlement.

The evolution of the mosque itself presents an important case study in symbolism in religious architecture. Based largely upon the plan of the Prophet's own house in Medina, the mosque served as a place of prayer (one of the five pillars of Islam) as well as acting as a social centre. Prayer was orientated towards the *qibla*, or the direction of the Shrine (*Kabbah*) at Mecca, which contained the holy black stone. As long as this fundamental pre-requisite was achieved, in practice any suitable space could be converted into a mosque. As a whole, the pattern of conversion of church buildings into mosques is a common theme across the early medieval eastern Mediterranean world and is best witnessed at Justinian's former church in Constantinople the Haghia Sophia. Internally, the spatial ordering requires little remodelling; the *qibla* provides for the axial spiritual focus of the building rather than an altar and church towers (where they exist) are easily converted into minarets. Symbolically, it is easier to reconfigure a Christian sacred place into a Muslim one than it is to convert a pagan sacred place. The temple was designed to be a house of a god, but the mosque or church does not carry such significance; the space is designed to be a meeting place, a layout designed to lead a congregation in a corporate act, a choreography of liturgy. However, places do retain a social memory of holiness and it is clear that the Arab incomers sought out places to build their mosques that did retain a degree of spiritual significance. Apart from the mosques, there are other sources to infer the presence of an Islamic community from a cultural-history perspective.

In Alexandria, the newly-arrived Arabs had the same problem that they had encountered elsewhere; they had to build important elements of their city into pre-existing classical ordered space. Additionally, the Arabs were open to other religions and were highly tolerant; they were not about to engage in a widespread spree of destruction of Christian or Jewish sacred places (contrast this with the behaviour of the Christian knights of the First Crusade in Jerusalem some 400 years later). But, importantly, the city was losing its position as a centre of secular power. Unlike other urban settlements in Islamic Egypt, such as the encampment at Fustat, the formation of discrete districts within the city (*khittas*) was forbidden at Alexandria; its loss of status is reflected by its description in early Arab historical sources as being nothing more than a *thagr* or frontier post. Alexandria still played a very important military role. Strategically the harbour was a valuable resource, and the Islamic navy was actually manned largely by Egyptian Christians (the city was used as a base for attacks on Byzantine outposts on Cyprus in 649, Rhodes in 672 and on Sicily in 651 and 669).

The urban space itself was reorganised within the existing city walls and as a general rule many churches were converted to mosques. This is especially true of the Melkite churches which were suffering politically under the new regime at the expense of the native Copts. Again the idea of seizing a sacred space was at once an economic necessity and an ideological one, although we can have no estimate of the rate of uptake of Islam in the city. Quite how many mosques would be needed for growing congregations is unclear, but one would envisage an initial phase where we may hypothesise that Islam was the faith of the rulers and military functionaries alone, whilst Christianity remained important for the urban masses. At the end of the twelfth century, some 400 years after the Arab conquest, historical sources mention the presence of a number of extant Christian monuments in Alexandria. We know from the writings of Abu Salih that the monasteries of the Enaton to the west of the city and the urban *Deir Asfal al-Ard* were still functioning, although their economic activities were scaled down considerably.[6] Five Coptic churches are mentioned (not by name) but four Orthodox (Melkite) foundations are described clearly. These are: St Sabas (the modern Greek Orthodox foundation), John the Baptist, St Nicholas, and St Mary.[7] Given the preferential treatment accorded to the Coptic Church under the domination of the Muslims, it is somewhat surprising that there are so many Melkite churches mentioned (and by name too). It is possible that the Melkites retained enough wealth, through their connections with international trade, in order to construct and maintain large and visually distinctive churches whilst the Copts, who were still essentially tied to the rural landscape, were less economically visible.

Three zones within the early Islamic city were defined; these were essentially semi-segregated zones, each surrounded by a wall. These are listed in contemporary documents as being: *Manna* (the Pharos area), *al-Iskandariyyah* (citadel area) and *Naqitah* (an unknown area). Later maps show that the medieval city had largely shifted its focus westwards, and was centred upon the area of land formed by silting around the heptasta-dion causeway;[8] it is clear that some of the most important mosques are located in this area rather than eastwards at the centre of the Ptolemaic and late antique city. The probable ninth-century 'mosque of a thousand columns' was usually identified with the site of the Church of Theonas in the north-west part of Minet el-Bassal; the mosque was not shaped like a basilica (we know this from contemporary accounts) and although it is possible that some spolia from the original church was used in its construction, it is probable that the original building was largely demol-ished. The mosque was damaged in 1798 and converted into a military hospital in 1884; a Franciscan monastery now stands on the site. The best description of the building comes from the early nineteenth-century French survey the *Description de l'Egypte* which tells of varied columns of different types of stone.

The Attarin Mosque is first recorded in 1084, but portions of the building dated, it was said, from the seventh century, making it arguably one of the earliest mosques to be built in Egypt,[9] although some sources do speak of two early mosques within Alexandria, a western mosque (unidentified) and an eastern one which may correspond to the Attarin mosque.[10] It is possible that the Attarin mosque occupied the site of the Great Church of Athanasius and, although it appears that some columns of the church may have been used, these have not survived, and, accord-ing to the surviving plans of the original (see *37*), the building does not seem to conform spatially to the characteristics of the original church.[11] The mosque was square and was built around a courtyard, although it was burnt down in 1830 and replaced by a new building in 1850. The build-ing we see today, whilst still retaining a frontage on the old east–west Canopic way (Horreya Street), now sits in a cramped corner location, a far cry from its earlier spacious incarnation (see *38*).

The mosque of Nabi Daniel bears witness to another form of syn-cretism of space, for here – apart from a possible earlier Christian significance – we have strong Ptolemaic associations. Tradition has it that this mosque, south of the intersection of Horreya and Nabi Daniel Streets, occupies the site of the old Ptolemaic *Soma*, the actual royal mausoleum of the Ptolemaic kings and also the physical burial place of Alexander the Great himself. The quest for Alexander's resting place has attracted a number of theories – some sound others less so – and it

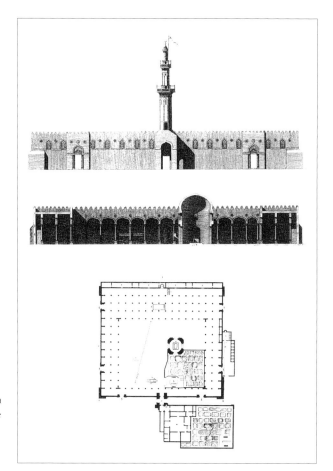

37 Plan and elevation of the Attarin mosque as reproduced in the *Description de l'Egypte (Antiquités)* Vol.V

should be no surprise that this place has attracted the attentions of 'professional' archaeologists and those of a more treasure-hunting persuasion. Excavations have taken place in the crypt, but nothing has been found of any significance, although the worshippers in the mosque above, or at least the few I have talked to there, secretly like the idea that Iskender al-Aqbar is buried beneath their mosque.

A number of Islamic cemeteries have been uncovered during the course of excavations around the city. One such was found in the Polish Kom el-Dikka excavations in 1999; in area MX a number of tombs were noted aligned on a SW–NE orientation (with head obviously pointing towards the *qibla*). These tombs have been dated, on the basis of Kufic inscriptions and imported ceramics, to around the eleventh-

38 The Attarin mosque in 2005. *Geoffrey Tassie*

39 The crypt of the mosque of Nabi Daniel. *Geoffrey Tassie*

twelfth centuries AD.[12] In addition to seeking out new zones for burial, the Islamicisation of wider space was accomplished through the establishment of extensive rural pilgrimage networks. The major pilgrimage route across the Alexandrian hinterland was without doubt the *Darb el-Haj al Maghreb*, a 2500km-long route (1600 miles) connecting the region of modern Algiers to Mecca.

The route itself was marked with a number of important wells and also bath houses; an eastern fork of the path took the pilgrim to Abu Mina (in common with many eastern Christian pilgrim centres, Islamic pilgrimage was also part of the biography of the site).[13] The custom of the 'moulid' ('birthday' in Arabic), visiting the tomb of a saint, was now highly popular, and attracted large numbers of pilgrims to special sites all over Egypt. The moulid was essentially a feast of a saint, albeit loaded with important secular connotations and they became part and parcel of everyday life in Islamic Alexandria where Muslims now renegotiated Christian sacred place. The Islamic moulid was similar to the Christian process of pilgrimage and sanctifying the place of the saint. Specialist buildings were erected over the tombs of the saint or holy man, this shrine or *Ziyara* would be the focus of the visit, and the experience of the moulid itself; this would be followed by a Quranic reading, a recitation of Sufic litanies, recitations of set formulae, processions and private ceremonies (such as circumcisions).[14]

Alexandria during early Islamic times was still a very cosmopolitan place. Within the social make up of the city we see a gradual trend towards the replacement of a Greek-speaking mercantile class by a Jewish one, reclaiming their former position that they had enjoyed under the Ptolemies. Trade was of course still important; finds of a variety of ceramics attest to far-reaching trade networks; Spanish, Italian, Byzantine, Syrian, Persian and Yemeni wares are all represented on archaeological sites of the early medieval period.[15] An account of a visit to Alexandria by a French nobleman in 1422, held in the Bodleian Library at Oxford, tells us something of the atmosphere in Alexandria at the end of the Crusades period.[16] The traveller notes the approach to the city and the relatively good state of the fortifications: 'exceedingly well fortified and secured all round with lofty walls'. No Christian ships may enter the 'old port' (which must mean the eastern harbour, Eunostos) but are free to come into the 'new port', i.e. the western harbour, the entrances to which is flanked by two mosques (not visible today; see also *40*). The traveller notes that the city 'is very long from east to west and narrow from south to north; it may be about six miles in circumference'; this would indicate that the city was occupying pretty much the original Ptolemaic space, although he does remark on the fact that the streets are in a bad state of repair. The city is still cosmopolitan, but now the mercantile class tend to be Italian rather than Greek, with particular mention made of Venetians, Genoese and Catalans. Now, on the wider stage, the political scene shifted again and a new dominant power arrived to seize power in Egypt. The Turks had arrived.

OTTOMAN CITY

In January 1517 a Turkish Ottoman army, moving southwards from Asia Minor, arrived in Egypt and defeated the Mamluk armies at Raydaniyya near Cairo. This momentous event ushered in a new period of prosperity for Egypt in general and Alexandria in particular. The Ottomans

40 A seventeenth-century French map of Alexandria. Two forts controlling access to the eastern harbour can be seen at bottom left; Pompey's pillar is visible at top right, outside the medieval city walls. Reproduced from G. Jondet (1921) *Atlas Historique de la Ville et des Ports d'Alexandrie,* Cairo: IFAO

retained a power base here, although a number of rebellious soldiers and Emirs were exiled in the city away from the centres of real political and military power.[17] Alexandria's urban space was reorganised again, with the Turks now moving their focus of habitation onto the area of the now silted heptastadion, away from the walled areas to the east. Alexandria remained outwardly cosmopolitan and trade was especially encouraged with the Venetians and with the western Mediterranean.

Religious differences within the New City were now recognisable – just as in Roman times – in terms of social status, spatial distribution and material culture;[18] *Dhimmis* ('people of the book', both Christians and Jews) as in earlier times were trusted with specific roles. Copts, for instance, were regarded as financial and administrative specialists. Different religious groups lived in specific quarters of the city; towards the end of Mamluk rule, for instance, the city's Jewish population was regarded with considerable distrust and they had to live in the citadel of Qait Bey, held as virtual prisoners and unarmed. Even the type of clothing one wore signified religious affiliation; in the 1580s Hadim Hasan Pasha ordered that Jews should wear the *taratir*, a conical red hat, whilst Christians should wear the *baranit*, a black hat. Ottoman Alexandria was not exactly noted for its religious tolerance; the confinement of the Jews shows indicates this mentality on the part of the city's rulers and even the Christians were not immune. Unwisely in 1577 the Christians attempted to erect a church over a mosque and Muslim cemetery, with monks (as usual) taking a very active role in the process of ethnic cleansing. This action was met with a violent sequel and as late as 1786 the Emir Murad Bey, in a fit of anti-Christian spite, ordered the demolition of the city's churches.[19] But the biography shifts again and soon new masters reshaped the idea and physical reality of Alexandria along the lines of their own myths and desires. The coming of Napoleon's armies in the late eighteenth century brought Alexandria a renewed, almost global recognition that has survived to this day.

EUROPEAN CITY REGAINED

The European geopolitical situation of the late eighteenth and early nineteenth century impacted upon Ottoman rule in Egypt. Napoleon, seeking to pressure Britain's strategic situation in India sought to expand into Egypt and although militarily this venture was ultimately unsuccessful, it did usher in essentially a new interest in the study of ancient Egypt and Alexandria. The major fruit of the French occupation was the compendious *Description de l'Égypte*, a multi-volume source that offers an exhaustive survey of Egypt: the antiquarian, the natural world, ethnology. The plate reproduced within this chapter (37) show just what a detailed work it was, produced as it was by Napoleon's military engineers and some of the finest minds of France. This tome marks the beginnings of modern Egyptology, its publication effectively almost coinciding with the transliteration of hieroglyphs by Champollion (the Rosetta stone had been found only a few miles up the coast) and a general awakening in the west of an interest in antiquity and antiquarianism. But Alexandria remained something of a political and aesthetic non-entity, lacking as it did the interest of the pharaonic remains further down the Nile. An interest of sorts in the history and remains of the city had been sparked on a small scale and following on from the fruits of successive European travellers, the bald picture was greatly extended and amplified with a survey conducted by Mahmud Bey in 1866. (Bey was an astronomer to the royal court, and the survey was finally published in Copenhagen in

1872 as *Mémoire sur l'Antique Alexandrie*. It remains an important scholarly resource.) With the opening of the Graeco-Roman Museum in 1892 and against a background of archaeological study driven by accidental finds during the course of development, we begin in the course of the nineteenth century to flesh out something of the archaeological nature of the city. From this point we may begin to talk about a separate and distinctive archaeology of Alexandria.

Away from this renewed interest in Alexandria's past, the place itself, shaking off the excesses of the Ottoman rule, began to re-attain some degree of cosmopolitan spirit under the dynamic rule of the Albanian Mohammed Ali, who remodelled parts of the city and improved the water supply.[20] For the first time in almost 2000 years a reinvigorated Greek settlement took place; the impetus for this new immigration was given by the arrival of the Tossizza brothers from Kevalla, and soon they were joined by wealthy, new professional and merchant classes. The new Greek community coalesced as the *'elleniki koinotis* (founded 1843) and were soon joined by a significant Italian and Albanian community, as well as Maltese and Armenians (the latter being ubiquitous traders across the Arab world). The Italian community was responsible for forming an administrative core, developing the museum and giving (architecturally) an Italianate architectural flavour to the new developments in the eastern suburbs. As in the early days of the City, it was almost as if these new ethnic communities formed a separate caste; there was a definite distinction between race and nationality retained amongst the Greeks, for instance, where being born in Egypt did not actually mean that one regarded oneself as being Egyptian. This idea was not far away from the original Alexandrian conception of Greek citizenship.

From this newly reinvigorated melting pot came writers and artists; one of the most recognisable names is the Alexandrian Greek poet Constantine Cavafy (1863-1933) who became famous in the wider literary world and for the first time, between the wars, we see the flowering of a truly Egyptian Alexandrian culture represented by the musician Sayed Darwisch and the painter Mahmud Said. Admittedly the exodus of Europeans after the Second World War impacted upon Alexandria's burgeoning cultural scene, yet Alexandria still retains an air of being at the cultural crossroads, more open and louche than the capital of Cairo, yet paradoxically more ordered and efficient. Alexandria has not lost its amazing capacity for reinvention.

ENVOI

So what can we take from this overview of changing spaces within one of the most famous cities of the east? From a methodological perspective we must be aware that the writing of any biography of changing urban spaces cannot be the preserve of a single discipline. The story of Alexandria demands to be told from a variety of perspectives, for this is more than a mere physical place, it is a more amorphous idea, a myth. Every strand of evidence presents its own problems. The archaeological picture alone, for instance, is especially problematic; with the rapid

41 The modern east–west road through the centre of the town, Horreya Street, respects the alignment of the earlier Ptolemaic Canopic way. *Geoffrey Tassie*

42 The remains of the original colonnaded Roman roadway beneath the modern level of Nabi Daniel Street. The picture is taken opposite the mosque of Nabi Daniel. *Geoffrey Tassie*

growth of Alexandria's urban space in recent years,[21] the importance of salvage and rescue archaeology cannot be underestimated. It is surely through chance finds rather than any structured research excavation that Alexandria will yield up more secrets of her past, but let us suspend belief for a moment and imagine what we could find if all the inhabitants left and we were able to peel back those many layers of physical deposit. This is an exercise more demanding than peeling back the historical layers formed by textual sources.

A number of compelling theoretical issues also present themselves. We set out at the beginning of the book with the hypothesis that changes in ideological values would be visible within the remodelling and re-conception of physical and imagined place and space in the city and its surrounding countryside. An implanted, almost alien Greek urban place changed the character of Egyptian space on a physical level (imposing spatial order) whilst maintaining and mixing key cultural elements of each civilisation. This is almost an ideal of religious and cultural syn-

43 Nineteenth-century town architecture. A shabby tenement block shows a meeting of southern European architectural tradition and the Islamic style of woodworking around the windows. *Niall Finneran*

cretism. The subsequent impact of Christianity was not merely a social shock of real magnitude; it too had profound effects upon the way that the city was organised. On a lesser scale (if only because we are yet to research the question in more depth) so too did the impact of Islam. If we have learnt anything from this study it is this: cultural and religious labels are easily generated and in many cases the sole way of recognising their presence in the archaeological record is to apply an arbitrary structured 'checklist' of traits to be ticked off. I believe that we have disabused that notion. Alexandria resists categorisation; it is, as we have suggested, a perfect conception of a postmodernist 'global village', a kaleidoscope of varied cultural histories and when dealing with such ideas we have to be more nuanced in our approach, abandon fixed boundaries of analysis and open our minds to the cosmopolitan syncretic outlook. This is surely why Alexandria still retains a fascination for the western mind. In the words of one scholar, the current artistic preoccupation with the city and its space retains an indelible thread of continuity. In Cavafy's poetry there is a sensuous link to the past, echoed also in Lawrence Durrell's works, depictions that play on light and shade rather like the technique of '*skiagraphia*' in Hellenistic art.[22] The thread and melange of social and cultural memory is strong in a place like Alexandria. Long may this schizophrenia continue to fascinate.

NOTES

Introduction

1 G. Sarton (1959) *A History of Science: Hellenistic Science and Culture in the Last Three Centuries* (Cambridge Mass.: Harvard University Press) p. 21.

2 For a study of Egypt's place in Africa, and a departure from the traditional Eurocentric, orientalist view, see A. Reid and D. O'Connor (eds.) (2003) *Ancient Egypt in Africa* (London: UCL Press).

3 C. Haas (1997) *Alexandria in Late Antiquity* (Baltimore: Johns Hopkins University Press) p. 6.

4 P. Fraser (1972) *Ptolemaic Alexandria* (three vols.) (Oxford: Clarendon Press).

5 C. Décobert and J-Y. Empereur (1998) (eds.) *Alexandrie Médiévale* (Cairo: I.F.A.O.).

6 The 1982 edition, published by Haag and with an introduction by Lawrence Durrell and notes by M. Haag is used throughout.

7 G. Durrell (1982) 'Introduction' in E.M. Forster (1982 ed.) p. xvi.

8 G. Durrell (1982) *ibid.* p. xi.

9 C. Haas (1997) *ibid.* p. 6.

10 J-Y. Empereur (1998) *Alexandria Rediscovered* (London: British Museum Press).

11 Before leaving this section, mention should be made of other core texts that have helped provide the background to this study, yet are not explicitly referenced herein. Any modern scholar of the history of Alexandria owes a considerable debt to the following sources which have also provided the scholarly bedrock for our studies:

A. Adriani (1966 edition) *Repertorio d'arte dell'Egitto Greco-Romano* (two vols.) (Palermo).

Mahmoud Bey (1872) *Mémoire sur l'Antique Alexandrie* (Copenhagen).

B. Tkaczow (1993) *Topography of Ancient Alexandria* (Warsaw: PWN).

Chapter 1: Situating Alexandria: historical, geographical and theoretical contexts

1 A. Bosworth (2000) 'Introduction' in A. Bosworth and E. Baynham (eds.) *Alexander the Great in Fact and Fiction* (Oxford: Oxford University Press) pp. 1–22.

2 M. Flower (2000) 'Alexander the Great and Panhellenism' in A. Bosworth and E. Baynham (eds.) *ibid.* pp. 96–135.

3   E. Friedrichsmeyer (2000) 'Alexander the Great and the kingship of Asia' in A. Bosworth and E. Baynham (eds.) *ibid.* pp. 136-166.

4   For a useful overview see P. Briant (1996) *Alexander the Great. The Heroic Ideal* (London: Thames and Hudson).

5   Dates after J. Finegan (1979) *Archaeological History of the Ancient Middle East* (Folkestone: Dawson).

6   Arrian, Alexander's biographer, gives an account in *Anabasis* (3: 1-4).

7   E. Friedrichsmeyer (2000) 'Alexander the Great and the kingship of Asia' in A. Bosworth and E. Baynham (eds.) *ibid.* pp. 136-166.

8   This 'culturally receptive environment' was cultivated by Alexander's successors; H. Hölbl (2001) *A History of the Ptolemaic Empire* (London: Routledge) p. 26.

9   H. Hölbl (2001) *ibid.* p. 77.

10 E.M. Forster (1982 ed.) *ibid.* p. 23.

11 After N. Davis and C. Kraay (1973) *The Hellenistic Kingdoms: Portrait Coins and History.* (London: Thames and Hudson); H. Hölbl (2001) *A History of the Ptolemaic Empire* (London: Routledge).

12 This is the most important of the Greek versions of the Old Testament; it differs from the Hebrew Bible in places, but was the standard version of the Old Testament until St Jerome's Vulgate of the late fourth century, a direct Latin translation of the Hebrew.

13 Siculus Diodorus *Bibliotheca Historia* (1972- ed. French; Paris: Les Belles Lettres).

14 After A. Bowman (1986) *Egypt After the Pharaohs* (London: British Museum Press).

15 After D. Talbot-Rice (1975 edition) *Islamic Art* (London: Thames and Hudson) p. 264.

16 Barbara Watterson points out that al-Siqilli means Sicilian and al-Rumi means Greek; he was therefore probably of *Christian* slave origin; B. Watterson (1997) *The Egyptians* (Oxford: Blackwell) p. 257.

17 A crucial distinction, and one which requires clarification. The schism dates back to AD 661, when the Khalif Ali (cousin of Mohammed) was assassinated, and his successor Muawiyah founded the Umayyad dynasty at Damascus; their high-handed rejection of the Islamic heritage of elected Khalifs brought them many enemies among the traditionalists. Among them were those who claimed to belong to the rightful tradition, the Shi'ia (party) of Ali. Sunni Muslims in turn saw themselves as the rightful heirs of the Islamic way of life (Sunnah).

18 L. Durrell 'introduction' in E.M. Forster (1982 ed.) p. ix.

19 M. El-Attar (1994) 'Egypt' in *Urbanisation in Africa; a Handbook* (Connecticut: Greenwood Press) pp. 165-180.

20 We will consider in a little more detail the archaeological evidence for Greek contact with Egypt in the time before Alexander the Great at the beginning of chapter 2.

21 J.D. Stanley, F. Goddio and G. Schnepp (2001) 'Nile flooding sank two ancient cities', *Nature* 412 (19.7 2001): 293-294.

22 This is provided by UNESCO, who has supported the project; see also the website of the library www.bibalex.gov.eg.

23 *Al Ahram Weekly* 17-23 October 2002, vol. 608.

24 Yet this museum is sadly and scandalously under-patronised; for the record it is located to the east of the city, on the first street on the right just before the new Stanley Bridge.

25 A. De Cosson (1935) Mareotis (London: Country Life) pp. 61 ff.

26 A. De Cosson (1935) *ibid.* p. 176.

27 The weakness of archaeology in attempting to reconstruct Alexandria's past is tackled in an important recent paper by Judith McKenzie (2003) 'Glimpsing Alexandria from archaeological evidence' *Journal of Roman Archaeology* 16: 35-61.

Chapter 2: Egyptian space, Greek place: the 'pagan city'

1   J. Boardman (1980 ed.) *The Greeks Overseas: Their Early Colonies and Trade.* (London: Thames and Hudson) p. 111; J. Milne (1939) 'Trade between Greece and Egypt before Alexander the Great' *JEA* 25: 177-183.

2   Strabo's *Geography* is the key contemporary account of the urban space of Alexandria. See *The Geography of Strabo* (trans. H. Hamilton and W. Falconer (1892)) three vols. (London: George Bell).

3   J-Y. Empereur (2002). *Alexandria: Past, Present, Future* (London: Thames and Hudson) p. 14. A useful appendix by John Baines in Judith McKenzie's paper (2003) 'Glimpsing Alexandria from Archaeological evidence' *Journal of Roman Archaeology* 16: 35-61 critically assesses the evidence for this idea.

4   P. Fraser (1972) *Ptolemaic Alexandria* (Oxford: Clarendon) pp. 5-6.

5   N. Lewis (1986) *Greeks in Ptolemaic Egypt* (Oxford: Clarendon) p. 8; P. Fraser (1972) *ibid.* p. 17.

6   J. Boardman (1980 ed.) *ibid.* p. 131.

7   J. Boardman (1980 ed.) *ibid.* p. 143.

8   H. Hölbl (2001) *A History of the Ptolemaic Empire* (London: Routledge) p. 26.

9   B. Kemp (1983) *Ancient Egypt: a Social History* (Cambridge: Cambridge University Press) p. 51.

10 I. Bell (1946) 'Alexandria ad Aegyptum' *Journal of Roman Studies* 36: 130-132.

11 R. Alston (2002) *The City in Roman and Byzantine Egypt* (London: Routledge) p. 2; R. Bagnall 'Landholding in late Roman Egypt: the distribution of wealth' *Journal of Roman Studies* 82: 128-149.

12 After his victory at the Battle of Actium in 31 BC, Octavian founded a new city – Nicopolis – to the east of the pre-existing city around the modern Ramleh area.

13 P. Fraser (1972) *ibid.* p. 3.

14 R. Bianchi (1993) 'Hunting Alexander's tomb' *Archaeology* 46/4: 54-56.

15 J. Pollitt (1986) *Art in the Hellenistic Age* (Cambridge: Cambridge University Press) p. 273.

16 Philo *In Flaccum* 64-71 (*Philonis Alexandrini In Flaccum* ed. H. Box (1939) (Oxford: Oxford University Press)); also see Strabo *ibid.* XVII 1-10.

17 P. Fraser (1951) 'A Syriac *Notitia Urbis Alexandrinae*' *JEA* 37: 103-108.

18 Possibly including private shrines as well as larger public ones.

19 L. Savile (1941) 'Ancient harbours' *Antiquity* 15: 209-232.

20 S. Kingsley (2001) 'Anatomy of the port of Alexandria' *Minerva* 12/4: 41.

21 See F. Goddio 'Underwater archaeological survey of Alexandria's Eastern Harbour' in M. Mostafa, N. Grimal and D. Nakashima (eds.) *Underwater Archaeology and Coastal Management: Focus on Alexandria,* (Paris: UNESCO) p. 60.

22 P. Fraser (1961) 'The Diolkos of Alexandria' *JEA* 47: 134-138.

23 The archaeologist David Knight of the University of Southampton has postulated that there was also a large foghorn to augment the light beam; the foghorn would have been built like a *hydraulus*, a water-driven musical instrument.

24 H. Frost (1975) 'The Pharos site, Alexandria, Egypt' *International Journal of Nautical Archaeology* 4/1: 126-130

25 H. Frost (1975) *ibid.* Marble is explicitly mentioned by Strabo in his *Geography* XVII: 1.6.

26 R. Goodchild (1961) 'The Helios on the Pharos' *Antiquaries Journal* 41: 218-223.

27 S. Handler (1971) 'Architecture on the Roman coins of Alexandria' *American Journal of Archaeology* 75: 57 – 74.

28 S. Handler (1971) *ibid.*

29 An Arab writer, Ibn al-Sayj, a sheikh of Malaga in Spain, visited the site in 1165 and wrote a description of the state of the Pharos in his *Kitab 'Alif Ba* which was finally published in Cairo in 1870. He notes that there is still a three-sectioned tower, the relative proportions being: first stage 31 fathoms height (one fathom equals six feet, or just less than two metres) the second being 15 fathoms in height and the final part being four fathoms in height. A mosque was built upon the apex. The total height of the structure in 1165 is given as 59 fathoms, or 107.9 metres. The dimensions of the Heptastadion, which must still have been visible above the silting, was given as 600 cubits length (348 metres), width 20 cubits (11 metres) and the roadway stood three cubits (1.7 metres) above the water level of the harbour. A viaduct 100 cubits (58 metres) in length made up the gradient at the end of the Heptastadion. See M. Asin and M. Otero (1933) 'The Pharos of Alexandria: summary of an essay in Spanish by Don Miguel de Asin with architectural commentary by Don M. Lopez Otero. Communicated by the Duke of Alba, Corresponding Fellow' *Proceedings of the British Academy* 19: 277-292.

30 J. Goudsmit and D. Brandon-Jones (2000) 'Evidence from the baboon Catacomb in North Saqqara for a west Mediterranean monkey trade route to Ptolemaic Alexandria' *JEA* 86: 111-119.

31 A. De Cosson (1935) *Mareotis* (London: Country Life) p. 65.

32 Herodotus *Persian Wars* II: 77: 3-5.

33 D. Crawford (1979) 'Food: tradition and change in Hellenistic Egypt' *World Archaeology* 11/2: 136-146.

34 P. Fraser (1972) *ibid.* p. 149.

35 R. Bagnall and B. Frier (1994) *The Demography of Roman Egypt* (Cambridge: Cambridge University Press) p. 54.

36 R. Bagnall and B. Frier (1994) *ibid.* p. 166.

37 R. Bagnall and B. Frier (1994) *ibid.* p. 177; R. and R. Alston (1997) 'Urbanism and the urban community in Egypt' *JEA* 83: 199-216.

38 J. Milne (1938) 'The currency of Egypt under the Ptolemies' *JEA* 24: 200-207.

39 A. Boyce (1949) 'Coins of Roman Alexandria' *Archaeology* 2: 181-183.

40 N. Davis and C. Kraay (1973) *The Hellenistic Kingdoms; Portrait Coins and History* (London: Thames and Hudson).

41 R. Bland (1996) 'The Roman coinage of Alexandria 30 BC- AD 296: interplay between Roman and local designs' in D. Bailey (ed.) *Archaeological Research in Roman Egypt* (Journal of Roman Archaeology Supplement Series 19) pp. 113-127; J. Milne (1943) 'Pictorial coin types of the Roman mint of Alexandria' *JEA* 29: 63-66.

42 R. Alston (2002) *ibid.* p. 187.

43 M. El-Abbadi (1962). 'The Alexandrian citizenship' *JEA* 48: 106-123.

44 P. Fraser (1972) *ibid.* p. 70.

45 See E. Naville (1890) *The Mound of the Jew and the City of Onias* (London: Egypt Exploration Fund).

46 A. Kerkeslager (1998) 'Jewish pilgrimage and Jewish identity in Hellenistic and early Roman Egypt' in D. Frankfurter (ed.) *Pilgrimage and Holy Space in Late Antique Egypt* (Leiden: Brill) pp. 99-228.

47 This problem is discussed in an excellent paper by Rachel Hachlili (2001) 'The Archaeology of Judaism' in T. Insoll (ed.) *Archaeology and World Religion* (London: Routledge) pp. 96-122.

48 An account is given in Josephus' *The Jewish War* (trans. G. Williamson 1959. London: Penguin Classics) 7; 412ff, for instance.

49 P. Modrezejewski (1991) *Les Juifs d'Egypte: de Ramses II à Hadrien* (Paris: Errance) p. 170.

50 G. Botti (1899) 'Etudes topographiques dans la Nécropole de Gabbari' *BSAA* 2: 37-56.

51 C. Clermont-Ganneau (1873) 'Ossuaire juif provenant d'Alexandrie' *Révue Archéologique* 26/ Series 2: 302-305.

52 P. Modrezejewski (1991) *ibid.* p. 67.

53 A. Kerkeslager (1998) *ibid.*

54 R. Alston (1997) 'Philo's *In Flaccum*: ethnicity and social space in Roman Alexandria' *Greece and Rome* 44: 165-175.

55 C. Haas (1997) *Alexandria in Late Antiquity* (Baltimore: Johns Hopkins University Press) p. 96.

56 C. Haas (1997) *ibid* p. 118.

57 C. Haas (1997) *ibid* p. 99 ff.

58 R. Finnestad (1998) 'Temples of the Ptolemaic and Roman periods: ancient traditions and new contexts' in B. Shafer (ed.) *Temples of Ancient Egypt* (London: I B Tauris) pp. 185-238.

59 H. Hölbl (2001) *ibid* p. 77

60 H. Hölbl (2001) *ibid* p. 111.

61 J. Pollitt (1986) *Art in the Hellenistic Age* (Cambridge: Cambridge University Press) p. 230.

62 J. Onians (1979) *Art and Thought in the Hellenistic Age: The Greek World View 350-50 BC* (London: Thames and Hudson) p. 24.

63 T. Fyfe (1936) *Hellenistic Architecture: An Introductory Study* (Cambridge: Cambridge University Press) p. 20.

64 J. Pollitt (1986) *ibid.* p. 238.

65 H. Holbl (2001) *ibid* p. 98.

66 G. Sarton (1959) *A History of Science: Hellenistic Science and Culture in the Last Three Centuries* (Cambridge Mass.: Harvard University Press) p. 18.

67 For a detailed site description based upon excavations in 1943-9 see A Rowe and B. Rees (1957) 'A contribution to the archaeology of the Western Desert' *Bulletin of the John Rylands Library* 39: 485-520.

68 S. Handler (1971) Ibid

69 P. Fraser (1972) ibid. pp. 276 ff.

70 R. Cribiore (2001) *The Gymnastics of the Mind: Greek Education in Hellenistic and Roman Egypt* (Princeton: Princeton University Press) p. 9.

71 R. Cribiore (2001) *ibid.* p. 22. The noted French scholar Champollion, who first translated Egyptian hieroglyphs, also observed syllabaries inscribed on the walls of Middle Kingdom tombs at Beni-Hassan, again they were presumably a kind of blackboard.

72 R. Cribiore (2001) *ibid.* p. 135.

73 G. Bushnell (1928) 'The Alexandrian Library' *Antiquity* 2: 196-204.

74 R. Macleod (2000) 'Introduction' in R. Macleod (ed.) *The Library of Alexandria* (London; IB Tauris) pp. 1-15.

75 According to Seneca, there were 400 000 volumes within both libraries, the smaller Serapeion library stocking 42 000 volumes. Josephus, in his *Antiquities* Book 7 Chapter 2, suggests a much lower figure of 200 000 volumes being held by both libraries (Bushnell 1928 *ibid*).

76 J. Onians (1979) *ibid.* p. 71.

77 J. Boardman (1980 ed.) *ibid* pp. 144 ff.

78 B. Fowler (1989) *The Hellenistic Aesthetic* (Bristol: Bristol Press) p. 44.

79 J. Pollitt (1986) *ibid* p. 59.

80 B. Fowler (1989) *ibid* p. 187; N. Himmelmann (1981) 'Realistic art in Alexandria' *Proceedings of the British Academy* 67: 193-207.

81 J. Pollitt (1986) *ibid*. p. 251.

82 R. Smith (1991) *ibid*. p. 17.

83 R. Smith (1991) *ibid*. p. 65.

84 R. Smith (1991) *ibid*. p. 210.

85 J. Pollitt (1986) *ibid*. p. 255.

86 W. Cockle (1984). 'State archives in Graeco-Roman Egypt from 30 BC to the reign of Septimus Severus' *JEA* 70: 106-122.

87 A. Bowman and D. Rathbone (1992) 'Cities and administration in Roman Egypt' *Journal of Roman Studies* 82: 107-127.

88 A. Bowman and D. Rathbone (1992) *ibid*.

89 A. Bowman (1986) *Egypt After the Pharaohs* (London: British Museum Press) p. 43.

90 D. Frankfurter (1998) *Religion in Roman Egypt: Assimilation and Resistance* (Princeton: Princeton University Press) p. 27.

91 R. Alston (1997) 'Ritual power in the Romano-Egyptian city' in H. Parkins (ed.) *Roman Urbanism: Beyond the Consumer City* (London: Routledge) pp 147-172.

92 A Rowe and B. Rees (1957) *ibid*.

93 D. Arnold (1999) *Temples of the Last Pharaohs* (Oxford: Oxford University Press) p. 138.

94 D. Arnold (1999) *ibid*. p. 264.

95 J. McKenzie (2003) 'Glimpsing Alexandria from Archaeological evidence' *Journal of Roman Archaeology* 16: 35-61.

96 J. McKenzie (1996). 'The architectural style of Roman and Byzantine Alexandria and Egypt' in D. Bailey (ed.) *Archaeological Research in Roman Egypt* (Journal of Roman Archaeology Supplement Series 19) pp. 128-42.

97 D. Bailey (1990) 'Classical architecture in Roman Egypt' in M. Henig (ed.) *Architecture and Architectural Sculpture in the Roman Empire* (Oxford: Oxford University Committee for Archaeology Monograph no. 29) pp. 121-137.

98 R. Alston (2002) *ibid*. p. 52.

99 M. Rodziewicz (1984) *Alexandrie III: Les Habitations Romaines Tardives d'Alexandrie* (Warsaw: PWN).

100 R. Alston (2002) *ibid*. p. 128 ff. Alston also notes the possible continuity of spatial organisation in the later development of the Cairene *Darb* or what the Americans would term the neighbourhood 'block'.

101 For an outline see M. Rodziewicz (1976) *Alexandrie 1: La Ceramique Romaine Tardive d'Alexandrie* (Warsaw: PWN).

102 T. Thomas (2000) *Late Antique Egyptian Funerary Sculpture* (Princeton: Princeton University Press) p. 3.

103 J. Pollitt (1986) *ibid*. p. 263.

104 J-Y. Empereur (1999) 'Alexandria: the Necropolis' *Egyptian Archaeology* 15: 26-28.

105 F. Hassan (ed.) (2002) *Alexandria: Graeco-Roman Museum: A Thematic Guide* (Cairo: Cultnat) p. 176.

106 F. Hassan (ed.) (2002) *ibid*. p. 185.

107 T. Fyfe (1936) *ibid*. p. 64.

108 H. Green (1986) 'The socio-economic background of Christianity in Egypt' in B. Pearson and J. Goehring (eds.) *The Roots of Egyptian Christianity* (Philadelphia: Fortune Press) pp. 100-113.

Chapter 3: Christianity and cosmopolitanism in late Antique Alexandria

1   R. Hutton (1999) *The Triumph of the Moon: A History of Modern Pagan Witchcraft* (Oxford: Oxford University Press) p. 4.

2   B. Pearson (1986) 'Earliest Christianity in Egypt: some observations' in B. Pearson and J. Goehring (eds.) *The Roots of Egyptian Christianity* (Philadelphia: Fortune Press) pp. 132-160.

3   R. Macmullen (1984) *Christianising the Roman Empire* (New Haven: Yale University Press) pp. 52 ff.

4   R. Bagnall (1993) *Egypt in Late Antiquity* (Princeton: Princeton University Press) pp. 261-268; G. Horsley (1987) 'Name change as an indicator of religious conversion in antiquity' *Numen* 34: 1-17.

5   See for example R. Fletcher (1997) *The Barbarian Conversion from Paganism to Christianity* (London: Harper Collins) p. 43; he quotes the example of how St Martin of Tours vigorously Christianised rural Gaul and destroyed a number of pagan installations in the process.

6   D. Montserrat and L. Meskell (1997) 'Mortuary archaeology and religious landscape at Graeco-Roman Deir el-Medina' *JEA*.

7   See D. Frankfurter (1998) *Religion in Roman Egypt: Assimilation and Resistance* (Princeton: Princeton University Press) p. 33

8   C. Haas (1997) *Alexandria in Late Antiquity* (Baltimore: Johns Hopkins University Press), p. 138

9   C. Haas (1997) *ibid.* p. 141.

10 C. Haas (1997) *ibid.* p. 151.

11 C. Haas (1997) *ibid.* p. 171

12 D. Frankfurter (1998) *ibid.* p. 221.

13 Plotinus was born in Egypt, but latterly settled in Rome. B. Russell (1991 ed.) *A History of Western Philosophy* (London: Routledge) p. 292.

14 R. Cavendish (1987) *A History of Magic* (London: Weidenfeld and Nicholson) p. 21.

15 There is no monolithic 'Gnostic' Christian heresy; the term covers a wide variety of Christian intellectual perspectives within the early Church. See H. Chadwick (1967) *The Early Church* (London: Penguin) pp. 33-37.

16 Archbishop Basilos (1991) 'Alexandrian Theology' in *CE vol. 1* pp. 103-4.

17 R. Alston (2002) *The City in Roman and Byzantine Egypt* (London: Routledge) p. 283.

18 After R. Alston (2002) *ibid.* pp. 287 ff.

19 A Rowe and B. Rees (1957) 'A contribution to the archaeology of the Western Desert' *Bulletin of the John Rylands Library* 39: 485-520.

20 C. Haas (1997) *ibid.* p. 207

21 A. Martin (1998) 'Alexandrie à l'époque romaine tardive: l'impact du Christianisme sur la topographie et les institutions', in C. Décobert and J-Y Empereur (eds.) *Alexandrie Médiévale* (Cairo: I.F.A.O.) pp. 9-21.

22 A. Martin (1998) Ibid

23 J. Gascou (1998) 'Les eglises d'Alexandrie' in C. Décobert and J-Y. Empereur (eds.) *Alexandrie Médiévale* (Cairo: I.F.A.O.) pp. 23-44.

24 N. Daoud (1997) 'Les sieges du patriarchat Copte d'Alexandrie' *Le Monde Copte* 27/8: 187-200.

25 After A. Atiya (1991) 'Historic Churches' in *CE* vol. 1, pp. 92-5; O. Meinardus (1997) 'Les débuts du Christianisme Alexandrin et les eglises d'Alexandrie' *Le Monde Copte* 27-28: 99-104.

26 J. Warren (1990) 'The first church of San Marco in Venice' *Antiquaries Journal* 70: 327-359.

27 For an overview see D. Chitty (1995 edition) *The Desert a City: An Introduction to the Study of Egyptian and Palestinian Monasticism under the Christian Empire* (Crestwood, New York: St Vladimir's Seminary Press); also A. Atiya (1980) *A History of Eastern Christianity* (Milwood, New York: Kraus Reprints) p. 61.

28 G. Gabra (2002) *Coptic Monasticism: Egypt's Monastic Art and Architecture* (Cairo: AUC Press) p. 21.

29 D. Frankfurter (1998) *ibid.* p. 3.

30 D. Frankfurter (1998) *ibid.* p. 277.

31 R. Gilchrist (1994) *Gender and Material Culture: The Archaeology of Religious Women* (London: Routledge).

32 R. Krawiec (2002) *Shenoute and the Women of the White Monastery* (Oxford: Oxford University Press).

33 S. Davis (1998) 'Pilgrimage and the cult of St Thecla in late antique Egypt', in D. Frankfurter (ed.) *Pilgrimage and Holy Space in Late Antique Egypt* (Leiden: Brill) pp. 303-329; see also C. Walters (1974) *Monastic Archaeology in Egypt* (Warminster: Aris and Phillips) p. 36.

34 For a useful overview of the origins and development of Egyptian monasticism see O. Meinardus (revised ed. 1999) *Monks and Monasteries of the Egyptian Desert* (Cairo: AUC Press).

35 P. Brown (1995) *Authority and the Sacred: Aspects of the Christianisation of the Roman Empire* (Cambridge: Cambridge University Press) p. 65

36 R. Markus (1990) *The End of Ancient Christianity* (Cambridge: Cambridge University Press) p. 163.

37 M. Dunn (2000) *The Emergence of Monasticism: From the Desert Fathers to the Middle Ages* (Oxford: Blackwell) p. 47

38 C. Haas (1997) *ibid.* p. 214.

39 M. Rodziewicz (1988) 'Remarks on the domestic and monastic architecture in Alexandria and surroundings' in E Van den Brink (ed.) *The Archaeology of the Nile Delta* (Amsterdam: N.S.A.O.E.) pp. 267-276.

40 M. Rodziewicz (1984) *Alexandrie III: Les Habitations Romaines Tardives d'Alexandrie* (Warsaw: PWN) pp. 198 ff.

41 M. Rodziewicz (1984) *ibid.* p. 211.

42 R. Coquin and M. Martin (1991) 'Dayr Qibriyus' in *CE* vol. 5: p. 850.

43 R. Coquin and M. Martin (1991) 'Monasteries in and around Alexandria' in *CE* vol. 5: pp. 1645-1646.

44 R. Coquin and M. Martin (1991) 'Dayr Asfal al-Ard' in *CE* vol. 5: pp. 782-783.

45 C. Haas (1997) *ibid.* p. 261.

46 E. Wipszycka (1994) 'Le monachisme Égyptien et les villes' *Travaux et Memoires* 12: 1-44.

47 M. Dunn (2000) *ibid.* p. 9.

48 C. Haas (1997) *ibid.* p. 324.

49 C. Haas (2002) 'John Moschos and late antique Alexandria' in J-Y Empereur and C. Décobert (eds.) *Alexandrie Médiévale* II (Cairo: I.F.A.O.) pp. 47-59.

50 M. Rodziewicz (1983) 'Alexandria and the District of Mareotis' *Graeco-Arabica* 2: 199-216.

51 A. Martin (1998) Ibid

52 A. De Cosson (1935) *ibid.*

53 C. Haas (1997) *ibid.* p. 261.

54 J. Gascou (1991) 'Enaton' in *CE* vol. 3: pp. 954-958.

55 In B. Evetts (translated and edited, 1895) *The Churches and Monasteries of Egypt and some Neighbouring Countries. Attributed to Abu Salih the Armenian.* (Oxford: Anecdota Oxoniensa/ Clarendon Press) p. 229.

56 J. Gascou (1991) 'Oktokaidekaton' in *CE* vol. 6: pp. 1826-7.

57 J. Gascou (1991) 'Eikoston' in *CE* vol. 3: pp. 951.

58 G. Monks (1953) 'The Church of Alexandria and the city's economic life in the sixth century.' *Speculum* 28: 349-362.

59 A. De Cosson (1935) *ibid.* p. 106.

60 H. Evelyn-White (1932) *The Monasteries of Nitria and Scetis* (New York: Metropolitan Museum of Art).

61 H. Evelyn-White (1933) *The Monasteries of the Wadi 'n Natrun* ((New York: Metropolitan Museum of Art).

62 C. Haas (1997) *ibid.* p. 258.

63 For an archaeological example see S. Coleman and J. Elsner (1991) 'The pilgrim's progress: art, architecture and ritual movement at Sinai' *World Archaeology* 26/1: 73-89.

64 D. Frankfurter (1998) 'Approaches to Coptic pilgrimage' in D. Frankfurter (ed.) *Pilgrimage and Holy Space in Late Antique Egypt* (Leiden: Brill) pp. 3-48.

65 Y. Volokhine (1998) 'Les déplacements pieux en Égypte pharoniques: sites et practiques culturelles' in D. Frankfurter (ed.) *Pilgrimage and Holy Space in Late Antique Egypt* (Leiden: Brill) pp. 51-97.

66 A. Kerkeslager (1998) 'Jewish pilgrimage and Jewish identity in Hellenistic and early Roman Egypt', in D. Frankfurter (ed.) *Pilgrimage and Holy Space in Late Antique Egypt* (Leiden: Brill) pp. 99-228.

67 Yi-Fu Taun (1977) *Space and Place: The Perspective of Experience* (London: Arnold) p.6 (cited by C. Tilley (1994) *A Phenomenology Of Landscape* (London: Berg) p. 14).

68 P. Grossmann (1998) 'The pilgrimage centre of Abu Mina', in D. Frankfurter (ed.) *Pilgrimage and Holy Space in Late Antique Egypt* (Leiden: Brill) pp. 281-302.

69 O. Meinardus (1962 edition) *Monks and Monasteries of the Egyptian Desert* (Cairo: AUC. Press) p. 356.

70 O. Meinardus (1962) *ibid.* p. 359.

71 D. Monserrat (1998) 'Pilgrimage to the shrine of SS Cyrus and John at Menouthis in late antiquity' in D. Frankfurter (ed.) *Pilgrimage and Holy Space in Late Antique Egypt* (Leiden: Brill) pp. 257-279.

72 T. Thomas (2000) *Late Antique Egyptian Funerary Sculpture* (Princeton: Princeton University Press) p. 3.

73 J-Y. Empereur (1999) 'Alexandria: the Necropolis' *Egyptian Archaeology* 15: 26-28.

74 T. Thomas (2000) *ibid.* p. 12.

75 J. Leibovitch (1939) 'Hellénismes et hébraïsmes dans une chapelle Chrétienne à el-Bagawat' *BSAC* 5: 61-68.

76 T. Thomas (2000) *ibid.* p. 59.

77 A. Badawy (1944) 'La persistence de l'ideologie et du formulaire païens dans le epitaphs Coptes' *BSAC* 10: 1-26.

78 G. Monks (1953) *ibid.*

79 E. Smirke (1867) 'Tin trade between Britain and Alexandria in the seventh century' *Journal of the Royal Institution of Cornwall* 2: 283-291.

80 M. Hollerich (1982) 'The Alexandrian bishops and the grain trade. Ecclesiastical commerce in late antique Egypt' *Journal of Economic and Social History of the Orient* 25/2: 187-207.

81 R. Bagnall (1993) *ibid.* p. 107

82 R. Bagnall (1993) *ibid.* p. 322.

83 R. Bagnall (1993) *ibid.* p. 290

84 M. Hollerich (1982) *ibid.*

85 D. Frankfurter (1998) *ibid.* p. 18.

86 D. Frankfurter (1998) *ibid.* pp. 40 ff.

87 D. Ainalov (1961) *The Hellenistic Origins of Byzantine Art* (ed. C. Mango; trans. E. and S. Sobolevitch) (New Jersey: Rutgers University Press) p. 25.

88 Y. Nessin Youssef (1990) 'La Christianisation des fêtes d'Osiris' *BSAC* 29: 147-152.

Chapter 4: Islamic Alexandria and beyond

1   There were a number of successive tented capitals upon the site of the Roman garrison centre of Babylon in Egypt (modern Coptic Cairo): al Fustat, then Al Askar, then Al Qatai and finally al-Qahira under the Fatimids in the late tenth century. The last named became the nucleus of Fatimid Cairo and henceforth the focus of the modern capital of Egypt.

2   P. Fraser (1991) 'Alexandria: Christian and Medieval' in *CE* Vol. 1: pp. 82-92. See also W. Kaegi (1995) *Byzantium and the Early Islamic Conquests* (Cambridge: Cambridge University Press).

3   See J. Haldon (1999) 'The idea of the town in the Byzantine Empire' in G. Brogiolo and B. Ward-Perkins (eds.) *The Idea and Ideal of the Town between Late Antiquity and the Early Medieval Ages* (Leiden: Brill) pp. 1-23.

4   T. Insoll (1999) *The Archaeology of Islam* (Oxford: Blackwell).

5   R. Hillenbrand (1999) ``Anjar and early Islamic urbanism' in G. Brogiolo and B. Ward-Perkins (eds.) *The Idea and Ideal of the Town between Late Antiquity and the Early Medieval Ages* (Leiden: Brill) pp. 59-98.

6   In B. Evetts (translated and edited, 1895) The Churches and Monasteries of Egypt and some Neighbouring Countries. Attributed to Abu Salih the Armenian. (Oxford: Anecdota Oxoniensa/Clarendon Press).

7   M. Martin (1998) 'Alexandrie Chrétienne à la fin du XIIe siècle' in C. Décobert and J-Y Empereur (eds.) *Alexandrie Médiévale* (Cairo: I.F.A.O.) pp. 45-49.

8   A. Hesse (1998) 'Arguments pour une nouvelle hypothèse de localisation de l'Heptastade d'Alexandrie' in J.Y. Empereur (ed.) *Alexandrina I* (Cairo: I.F.A.O.) pp. 21-34.

9   The earliest is held to be the Mosque of 'Amr Ibn al-'As, founded at Fustat in c. AD 641. D. Behrens-Abuseif (1989) *Islamic Architecture in Cairo: an Introduction* (Leiden: Brill).

10 D. Behrens-Abuseif (2002) 'Topographie d'Alexandrie médiévale' in J-Y Empereur and C. Décobert (eds.) *Alexandrie Médiévale* II (Cairo: I.F.A.O.) pp. 113-126. The location of 'Amr's own mosque, described as being on a hill, is not known.

11 See B. Tkaczow (1993) *The Topography of Ancient Alexandria* (Warsaw: Polish Academy of Science) p.78.

12 G. Majcherek (2000) 'Kom el-Dikka excavations 1999/2000' *Polish Archaeology in the Mediterranean* 12: 23-34.

13 A. De Cosson (1935) *Mareotis* (London: Country Life Books) p. 126.

14 M. Winter (1992) *Egyptian Society under Ottoman Rule 1517-1798* (London: Routledge) p. 181.

15 V. François (1998) 'Les céramiques médiévales d'Alexandrie: un témionage archéologique' in C. Décobert and J-Y. Empreur (eds.) *Alexandrie Médiévale* (Cairo: I.F.A.O.) pp. 57-64.

16 J. Webb (1827). 'A survey of Egypt and Syria undertaken in the year 1422 by Sir Gilbert de Lannoy Knt. Translated from a manuscript in the Bodleian Library at Oxford' *Archaeologia* 21: 281-444.

17 M. Winter (1992) *Egyptian Society under Ottoman Rule 1517-1798* (London: Routledge) p. 68.

18 M. Winter (1992) *ibid*. pp. 212 ff.

19 M. Winter (1992) *ibid*. p. 220.

20 P. Fraser (1981) 'Alexandria from Mohammed Ali to Gamal Abdul Nasser' in G. Grimm, H. Heinen and E. Winter (eds.) *Alexandrien: Aegyptiaca Trevensia* (Mainz: Von Zabern) pp. 63-74.

21 Between 1976 and 1986, the latest figures to hand, the city grew 2-3%; the population now is estimated to be *c*.4 million, making Alexandria a very dense population centre.

22 B. Fowler (1989) *The Hellenistic Aesthetic* (Bristol: Bristol Press) p. 195. Skiagraphia is a technique associated with the Athenian painter Apollodorus *(fl.* 400 BC) and put simply it means the use of shading to render shape and mass. Apollodorus' surname was Skiagraphos, which means 'shader'. In a more modern sense this sentiment is recalled by a delightful legend painted upon a traffic bridge on the main route leading south from the city: 'Alexandria is a love wave breaking upon Egypt's land'.

INDEX

References in bold refer to illustrations

If you are interested in purchasing other books published by Tempus,
or in case you have difficulty finding any Tempus books in your local bookshop,
you can also place orders directly through our website

www.tempus-publishing.com